Give Yourself a PEP TALK

This book was donated by CHOICES for Parents/ Chicago Hearing Society to encourage literacy for persons with hearing loss. For more information please call us at 866.733.8729 or visit us at www.CHOICESforParents.org.

Give Yourself a PEP TALK

Joan Marie Galat

PELICAN PUBLISHING COMPANY
Gretna 2013

Copyright © 2013
By Joan Marie Galat
All rights reserved

The word "Pelican" and the depiction of a pelican are trademarks of Pelican Publishing Company, Inc., and are registered in the U.S. Patent and Trademark Office.

Library of Congress Cataloging-in-Publication Data

Galat, Joan Marie, 1963-
  Give yourself a pep talk / by Joan Marie Galat.
     p. cm.
  ISBN 978-1-4556-1785-2 (pbk. : alk. paper) — ISBN 978-1-4556-1795-1 (e-book) 1. Self-talk. 2. Self-esteem. 3. Self-acceptance. 4. Motivation (Psychology) I. Title.
  BF697.5.S47G35 2013
  158.1— dc23

2012036716

Printed in the United States of America
Published by Pelican Publishing Company, Inc.
1000 Burmaster Street, Gretna, Louisiana 70053

To those who need to escape from emotional places of solitude and despair

Contents

Preface 11
Introduction: Living with Unsolved Problems 13

Emotional Honesty

Stop Thinking "Always" and "Never" 17
Find the Courage to Be Honest with Yourself 18
Acknowledge That Some Things Are Understood through
    Emotion 19
Recall Events with Accuracy 20
Consider Emotional Support As Important As Financial
    Concerns 21
Recognize What Is Achievable 22
Discover the Purpose of Your Feelings 23
Turn Worries into Troubleshooting Plans 24
Deal with Knowledge Instead of Opinion 25
Refuse to Be Hostage to Past Hurts 26
Generate Factual Stories 27
Train Yourself to Stop Negative Thoughts 28

Hope and Acceptance

Accept That You Are Human 29
Manage Your Regrets 30
Accept That Friends Will Come and Go from Your Life 31
Forgive Yourself for Making Mistakes 32
Learn to Appreciate Yourself 33
Remember That Everything That Has a Beginning Has
    an End 34
Cope with the Future by Understanding the Past 35
Allow Yourself Time to Feel 36
Accept Your Disabilities 37
Consider Whether Your Expectations Are Reasonable or
    Fair 38
Acknowledge Sorrow 39

Conscientious Living

Define Your Dreams and Map How You Are Going to Achieve
  Them 41
Focus on Blue Skies Instead of Thunderclouds 42
Enjoy Your Own Story 43
Look for the Reward When Something Bad Happens. 44
Do a Kindness Every Day 45
Exercise Your Brain.................................... 46
Consider Whether the Annoying Things People Do Really
  Matter 47
Answer Your Social Conscience.......................... 48
Deliberately Refocus Your Thoughts 49
Analyze Those You Admire 50
Look for Positive Signs................................. 51
Apply Judgment before Offering Help 52
Respond with Dignity................................... 53
Forgive Those Who Fail You 54

Practical Matters

Keep Fewer Dishes Rather Than Buying More Cupboards 55
Define a Fair Level of Control 56
Tackle the Achievable 57
Anticipate Change..................................... 58
Reduce Stress through Physical Activity 59
Consider Whether You Talk about Something Too Often 60
Use Adversity to Examine Priorities 61
Enjoy What You Can Control 62
Make a Business Plan for Life 63
Support Yourself....................................... 64
Prevent a Crisis 65
Put On Your Own Oxygen Mask First..................... 66
Refocus Your Attention 67
Work to Develop Fulfilling Activities..................... 68
Get Some Air 69
Brainstorm for Possibilities 70
Know When to Seek Help 71

Identity and Perception

Avoid Surrounding Yourself with People Who Continually and
    Deliberately Hurt You 73
Recognize That People Tend to Behave Poorly When They
    Feel Badly 75
Accept That Nobody Can Read Your Mind 76
Know That Failure Means You Are Trying................77
Ease Away from Destructive Self-Preoccupation 78
Use Gracious Thoughts to Nurture Peaceful Feelings 79
Embrace the Unpredictable............................80
Consider the Different Roles You Play....................81
Liberate Your Thinking 82
Imagine How You Would Help Someone with the Same
    Problem 83
Pay Attention to Recurring Messages....................84
Choose Your Orbit 85
Distinguish between Dreams to Pursue and Dreams to Enjoy in
    Thought 86
Appreciate Your Individuality 87
Choose Which Experiences Define You...................88
Live in Reality.......................................89
Be Aware of Your Points of Influence....................90

Meaningful Days

Do Not Schedule Every Minute of Your Time...............91
Accumulate Meaningful Experiences.....................92
Give Worries the Day Off..............................93
Nurture Your Sense of Humor 94
Do Not Waste Time Trying to Win Over Those Who Do Not Want
    You for a Friend..................................95
Give Your Nights to the Sandman........................96
Do Something for Yourself Every Day 97
Question the Routines in Your Life 98
Make Lists and Start Small 99
Give Yourself the Gift of Time 100
Use Setbacks to Your Advantage 101

Build Anticipation into Your Life........................102
Keep Yourself Occupied 103
Celebrate Progress As Much As Achievement..............104

Clear Communication

Define Your Feelings with the Right Words 105
Practice the Art of Conversation 106
Choose Success over Revenge 107
Take Risks to Grow 108
Define Your Motivations...............................109
Incorporate Genuine Compliments into Communication 110
Define What Success Means to You......................111
Give Up the Need to Be Right 112
Record Your Personal Stories..........................113
Nurture Creative Thinking.............................114
Speak Up..115
Be Wary of How You Interpret Text 116
Practice Active Listening..............................117
Stop Making Excuses..................................118
Live an Inspiring Life 119

Next Steps 120

Preface

There was a time when I would have described myself as someone who could take things in stride. I didn't know that I had never been truly challenged. My reliable, positive outlook on life began to collapse when a large number of things went wrong in a short period. Every time that it seemed as if I might begin to recover and move forward out of conflict, another hit saw me waver.

The difficulties first began with the breakdown of my seventeen-year marriage. A painful divorce followed, exacerbated by unexpected judgments. Even though it might be good to find out who your friends are, it certainly is not fun. The next jolt—a disastrous relationship—saw my self-esteem flounder. It became difficult to concentrate on the things that I needed to do. And as stress can contribute to illness, I soon experienced assorted medical ailments and two surgeries.

Following recovery, I found myself facing the most unexpected and painful challenges—one of these, an estrangement—that I will never stop hoping to repair.

Family and friends tried to be supportive, but it is very hard for others to know how to handle intense, living grief. When not in the midst of an "incident," I succeeded in appearing cheerful around others—provided that they didn't raise the wrong topics. But the effort took an enormous amount of energy. A pervading sense of loneliness and isolation magnified my existence. My emotional state was that of all-encompassing despair, with waves of sadness, pain, and anger sweeping all optimism from my mind. I had no reason to believe that my life would improve.

Yet sometimes, between these overriding, black, oppressive periods, I did experience brief moments of ease. At these times, I could look at my situation with a clearer perspective, and that is when hope became an option.

As an author, I had developed the habit of writing down my ideas. In this difficult period, I used that practice to learn to overcome my frustration. I tried to define my thoughts well enough to pinpoint from where the good feelings originated. The words I collected sparked optimism and nurtured calm. I recognized that even fleeting relief is worth pursuing. I hoped that good moments could grow into hours or even days.

Finally, I found a benefit to my haphazard scribbling on the closest piece of paper and habit of letting my notes stack up in random piles. When despair blossomed, I tended to clean and organize my house, at which point I happened upon my insights, right when I needed them most. These notes came to represent my own personal pep talks. I began to depend on them as practical tools to displace my negative outlook.

I share this brief background because I feel that it is important for you, the reader, to know the weight of my own experience with challenging emotions and situations. Yes, I know depression. Yes, I know stress. But yes, I have found ways to cope. The despair I endured could have broken me. But I'm still here, functioning—doing well—in the ways that I have come to measure success.

It is my wish that you will use the vignettes on the following pages as thoughts to hold on to when overwhelmed with tides of hopeless, desperation, sadness, and the certainty that things will never get better. I hope that you will build an escape from your emotional solitude and despair by embracing the ideas most relevant to your situation. Despite the magnitude of your struggles, nurture hope knowing that these strategies evolved from a place of suffering into one of new possibilities. May these pep talks help you find fresh strategies to renew the joy in your life and lead you to find contentment despite the tremendous hardship of living with overwhelming difficulties.

Introduction:
Living with Unsolved Problems

Sometimes you lose your way. You make unbelievable mistakes. You take a risk that does not pay off. Life crises and unexpected events chip and shatter the vulnerable parts of your soul. Pain smolders, simmers, and flares in increments too small to measure, building into something much larger than the sum of its parts. No matter the challenge, it can feel like the ability to function at your best is slipping away. Sometimes, it may feel as if you have lost the ability to act at all.

Time feels wasted when you are overwhelmed, and periods of feeling distracted, depressed, morose, irritable, angry, guilty, tired, lonely, or misunderstood only seem to grow. Self-esteem takes an extended holiday. Any former ability to face life with a positive outlook is on leave. Strategies that once helped you cope no longer work, and you are so very tired. No matter how hard you try, there does not seem to be any way to relieve these overpowering feelings. Life becomes a burden to bear instead of a joy to experience.

When something deep inside reacts to life's kicks with ongoing despair, you have to learn a trait that does not come naturally: the ability to live with unsolved problems.

Only you know what this entails for yourself as an individual. This could mean anything from accepting to letting go to confronting the trials that torment you. If you have acted in ways you regret, it may require teaching yourself to leave guilt behind. If you are stuck in a pattern in which you dwell on self-defeating critical thoughts, it will be necessary to train yourself to appreciate yourself. If you berate yourself for giving into despair or consider yourself weak for not feeling strong enough to pull yourself out of a slump, you will need to find a way to forgive yourself for being human instead of the impermeable superhero of your imagination—refusing to forgive your own imperfections only fuels emotional pain. Living with unsolved problems can also mean forgiving others when you feel victimized. It may not sound very appealing at the moment, but forgiveness offers the most direct path to moving on and conquering what holds you back.

You can begin the process to lessen stress and depression's debilitating impacts by learning to recognize that every emotion—pleasant and unpleasant—is a part of being human. Even suffering is natural. Despite the strength of your desire, you cannot avoid emotional reactions to different upsetting experiences or always be strong when coping and rising above obstacles both petty and large. No matter how it appears, no one is built with that kind of control and neither are you. Does that mean you should accept suffering and give up? No, not at all. You should accept that you are not a lesser being for succumbing to pain. At the same time, you must realize that you also have a responsibility to respect yourself and do what it takes to be as well as possible, both physically and mentally.

When emotional health is poor, it is necessary to rule out medical causes that might aggravate your condition. Physical and mental check-ups with your doctor are integral components to tackle emotional health and regain stability in your life.

If your doctor confirms the symptoms of depression, you may wonder if it indicates that something is wrong with your character and rationalize that since you have free will, you should be able to snap out of it. In fact, some people may offer you this unhelpful advice. Instead, recognize and accept that depression is a medical condition and not a character flaw. You cannot suddenly choose to be happy any more than you can choose not to have high blood pressure or a broken leg. If, on top of all your other melancholy feelings, you feel guilty about feeling depressed, remember that having a medical condition is not your fault. However, to ensure proper diagnosis and treatment, you do have the responsibility to seek medical attention should you require it. Results take time but can be achieved.

Take care of your physical health while learning to help yourself emotionally. It is my experience and belief that a depressed person can accelerate the healing process by learning to restructure patterns and approaches to thinking. Working on strengthening your physical health at the same time as your mental health will provide mental balance and an overall makeover.

However, there is still one big obstacle. In theory, you have the ability to change your thinking and alter your habits. In reality, depression takes away your desire to make this effort and the faith you need in yourself to get started. Rather than using this knowledge as a license to give up, your solution lies in accepting that the path you travel will be maneuvered in small steps. Grand, sweeping changes are not practical to maintain or likely to succeed in the long term. Small steps take time but will get you where you want to go.

Now you are ready to find your way. Use this book to nurture reassurance and find new perspectives. Establish the habit of reading a pep talk in the morning and contemplating it throughout the day. Examine how it relates to how you spend your time and how you interact with the people in your life. When the opportunity arises, explore the outlooks that especially intrigue you by discussing your impressions with others. Remind yourself that no matter what outside factors affect you and your goals, you will be able to make increments of effort. Take modest steps until you feel ready to tackle larger challenges. Be proud of your progress along the way. Look forward to rising out of your shadowy place of suffering, for you will surely reach a new plateau where you can feel content and grow into your own unique potential.

It takes time to change the habits that form when despair takes hold—but it is not impossible. The following pages can help you find your way out of frustration and desperation to an emotionally healthy place of self-appreciation and pride. Begin with a pep talk. Focus on developing an outlook that initiates self-respecting changes. But most of all, look forward to experiencing and living with hope—and know that your persistence will ensure that you arrive!

Emotional Honesty

Stop Thinking "Always" and "Never"

Overcoming depression is difficult. I did not understand it before I experienced it anymore than I knew what it was like to raise a child before I gave birth. Depression can isolate and debilitate.

—Joan Marie Galat

When thinking in the negative, it is easy to think of a situation in terms of "always" or "never": "I will always be unhappy" or "I will never solve this problem." The tendency to distort general thoughts into negative mantras is a debilitating habit.

Escape discouraging feelings and statements by replacing them with more accurate and positive truths. For example, instead of thinking, "I have a complete lack of willpower when it comes to food," reanalyze your situation: "I may have quit lifting weights, but I'm eating more healthy foods." Replace "I can't follow directions" with "Once in a while I do get lost, but often I find my way on the first try." When you make a mistake, do not berate yourself. Instead, realize, "Sometimes I'm right, but sometimes I'm wrong, just like everyone else in the world."

Listen to the language of your thoughts and make an effort to examine what is fact and what constitutes negative exaggeration. Choosing to distinguish between the truth of your circumstances and pessimism will give you the benefit of a more realistic perspective. Remind yourself that "always" and "never" thoughts rarely reflect genuine circumstances and that all situations change with time.

Find the Courage to Be Honest with Yourself

Truly loving yourself means treating yourself with honesty and respect. It means accepting responsibility for your actions. It means making a sincere effort to solve problems rather than taking the easy way out by complaining or reproaching others when things do not work out the way you expect.

Instead of blaming someone else when things go wrong, envision the other person's perspective and encourage him or her to do the same for you. The fastest way to relieve your own frustration is often to soothe the other person's first, because it reaffirms open lines of communication. When appropriate, you can accomplish this without losing face by saying something similar to "It wasn't my intention to upset you or give the impression that your feelings don't matter."

This type of language helps deflate the other person's anger and prevents what is often trivial from escalating into something extreme. Try not to be the child with the knee-jerk reaction, shouting "wasn't me" every time something goes wrong. Instead, nurture yourself by finding the courage to be honest about your present situation and how you came to be at this point.

Acknowledge That Some Things Are Understood through Emotion

While experience, education, religious outlook, and logic shape beliefs and opinions, your convictions also arise from less-definable emotional impressions. Your subconscious communicates in a way that language cannot. Gut instinct confirms perceptions that your mind might choose to rationalize away. Rather than attempting to verbally defend your way of thinking, acknowledge and accept that some things are best grasped through emotion.

Sometimes, you will find that the passage of time and new experiences prove that some situations are not as they first appeared. What you think you know may be incorrect; what you feel but find difficult to explain can be right. The certainties you once held as facts may dissolve into puddles of doubt. Gray can enter situations once judged black and white. Long-held opinions might become cloudy if you seek to develop perspectives that encompass emotional understanding as well as crucial facts.

Human maturation involves recognizing when your impressions are justified and when they are unfounded. Beware of lightly dismissing your emotions, for some experiences are first understood by feeling.

Recall Events with Accuracy

The human memory tends to focus on certain facts and dismiss others depending on opinion or mood. When you remember events, make an extra effort to recall them fairly. For example, it is easy to reflect on all of the good things about a relationship when missing someone and just as easy to dwell on all of the bad things that they did when feeling angry. It may be natural to remember the carefree days of your childhood, but it is inaccurate to forget the worries of youth.

Save yourself from undeserved guilt or disproportionate despair by engaging honesty as you examine both the good and bad aspects of your life. Be aware of the inaccuracies of selective memory and, if necessary, console yourself with these facts: you have learned valuable lessons, you are more self-aware, you will be able to help others with this experience, you tried your best, and you will know to try different approaches if ever faced with similar situations.

Consider Emotional Support As Important As Financial Concerns

Strive to maintain a happy equilibrium between the time you allot to keep up with daily duties and the time you spend nurturing your most cherished relationships. How you spend your hours will determine the memories you make. Do not wait for a personal crisis or catastrophe to force you into examining your priorities such as repairing an estrangement, rebuilding a friendship, or reestablishing what is precious. Accept that giving emotional attention to yourself and to those dear to you is just as important as financially supporting yourself and your family.

Recognize What Is Achievable

There are very few things in life of which you can be sure. Because guaranteed outcomes are unlikely, it is important to recognize which situations are worthy of your effort and which ones are best put aside. When you accept that there are areas in which you have little or no power, you do not need to worry about as many things. This acknowledgement and acceptance frees you to devote time and energy to matters in which you can make the most difference.

Discover the Purpose of Your Feelings

Emotions are guideposts that help you respond to circumstances around you. Your reactions to current situations, as well as gut instinct and moral perspective, are influenced by past experience. Feelings can be difficult to control. Therefore, you should be wary of how you let initial responses direct your emotions or opinions. At the same time, be kind to yourself. Do not judge your emotions as good or bad, right or wrong. What matters is how you choose to interpret your feelings and their consequences. For example, fear is constructive when it helps you avoid a real danger, such as walking on thin or black ice. However, a destructive fear or paranoia might cause an overreaction, such as refusing to walk outside during the winter.

Responding to emotions in healthy ways involves knowing how to manage your reactions. To achieve appropriate control, examine what positive outcomes your feelings could have. Anger and pain indicate that something around you is hurtful; once you identify its cause, you can address the issue. Shame and guilt indicate wrongs that need to be set right. Sadness often buds from missed opportunities. Pay attention to these guideposts, because they are the stop signs that will allow you to pause and reflect on areas of discontent and how to better your situation. You are the only person who honestly can evaluate your circumstances and feelings.

Turn Worries into Troubleshooting Plans

Worry is natural. Imagining potential scenarios can help you to make smart decisions as you consider both positive and negative possibilities. However, concerns that are excessive, intrusive, and persistent leave you both mentally and physically worn out and can wind up consuming you. To reduce the helplessness that accompanies worry, divert your energy into troubleshooting the most promising solution by writing down your options. As you explore ideas, cross off the choices that are least likely to improve your outcome. This strategy defines the spectrum of possibility while narrowing your focus towards the productive.

Define your fears, rate the likelihood of them occurring, and list possible responses and solutions. Realize that some situations are more manageable than others. Some concerns may be truly unfounded. Some might make you laugh now that they're listed in black and white. The act of writing down your fears helps define the levels at which they exist and whether each one is justified or futile. It also provides a forum for self-examination by exploring negativity and apprehensions. Review your list when you find yourself rehashing solutions that you've already considered. Limit unnecessary worries and turn obstacles into productive troubleshooting sessions.

Deal with Knowledge Instead of Opinion

It can be incredibly easy to reach an opinion regardless of whether you have all of the facts. When choosing sides, differentiate between impressions and truths.

Knowledge, at its base, is truth gathered through fact and reasoning. There is no room for speculation, assumption, inference, or guessing. The next time that you are inclined to pass judgement or make a decision, consider whether you are reacting to feelings or truths. Make a deliberate effort to sift rumors, insinuations, and suppositions out of your decision.

A lively conversation may compel you to commit to a certain outlook, but resist the urge to give in before you have gathered all of the facts. If you find yourself in a difficult position, take the time to reason through what you know and what you need to find out. It is best to wait before answering instead of giving a hurtful or inconclusive response. Searching for knowledge will spare you from the stress of making statements that you have not thought through.

Refuse to Be Hostage to Past Hurts

Whether remembered or forgotten, everything you experience contributes to how you think and behave. Some painful events can be shrugged off months or years later without a second thought. Some incidents are much harder to shake.

While time is your best friend when it comes to letting things go, do you really want to see two, five, or ten years pass before finally moving on? Even if you feel that you are not "over" something, you can refuse to be hostage to past hurts. You will know that you have processed the situation or issue enough when the conversations in your head continuously lead to the same conclusions. When that time comes, tell yourself to stop and let go of your resentment. Accept the experience as one of life's learning events, something unfortunate that happened but that is now in the past. It may have been destructive, painful, or unfair, but you have survived and emerged wiser and more resilient.

Generate Factual Stories

Suppose you anticipate a visitor who never arrives. Depending on the situation and your outlook, the incident might generate resentment, despair, or self-pity. On the other hand, you may find yourself feeling more charitable, grateful, or relieved. Perhaps you regretted making the commitment. Because the mind looks for relationships between emotions and experiences, your response will depend on which feelings you assign to the event. The associations you make between fact and feeling become part of the storyline your mind creates to make sense of what happens.

If your response to being stood-up is "How self-centered! She thinks I have nothing better to do," then you have taken the facts personally—you have allowed your feelings to control your perspective. Reacting to feelings instead of information triggers unrealistic attitudes and expectations. It inserts a devious plot into your story where perhaps none exists. Remember, this scenario contains only one fact: the expected visit did not take place. Your perception of the situation changes as your associations change. If you think, "She probably didn't show up because traffic is so backed-up. It has nothing to do with me as a person," then your mental report would be more objective.

Note that both stories are contrived. Neither reflects a known truth, though the second is clearly a more gracious reaction. The next time that your mind gets inventive generating a plot, laugh and appreciate your imagination at work—but don't indulge in impulsive reactions or deprecating speech in response to the judgements and conclusions that attach themselves to your feelings. Instead, return to the facts, examine what you know in order to keep a firm grip on the truth, and only generate factual stories.

Train Yourself to Stop Negative Thoughts

If happiness depended on a high standard of living, many therapists and spiritual advisers would be out of work. After basic needs are met, thinking is the most significant factor that determines the quality of your life. How you feel and respond to experience is in direct correlation with how you think.

With effort and practice, you can enhance your outlook by training yourself to stop onslaughts of negative thoughts. When depressing, unconstructive, disobliging notions burrow through your mind, eliminate them by changing your vocabulary. Replace "It's impossible" with "There must be a way." Swap "I don't get it" for "I need more time to figure it out." Change "I'm not good at that" to "I don't have to be good at everything." Restructure negative inclinations to generate a positive outlook.

Be attentive to how your thoughts dictate your mood and challenge the validity of negative perspective. Accept that you have shortcomings, and appreciate your strengths rather than bemoaning your limitations.

Hope and Acceptance

Accept That You Are Human

One important step to gaining peace of mind is learning to accept that you cannot have everything you want and that you cannot always arrange circumstances to suit your ideal situation. When you believe that you should have something, you have the responsibility to determine how to go about getting it and the duty to let go of the idea if it does not turn out to be sensible or plausible. There is no benefit to making excuses to yourself or others, especially if you have not acted on your goals. Nothing is gained from complaining about how life is unfair or bemoaning that a dream is out of reach. Because you are a human being rather than a perfect being, fulfilling a personal desire is a goal that sometimes you will obtain and other times you will not. The only failure is the one that involves not trying. Do your best to accept that you are human and give your best effort at every opportunity.

Manage Your Regrets

Help yourself manage emotional or distressing events from the past by allowing time to experience a reasonable mourning period in proportion to the episode. Giving yourself the opportunity to express grief over a situation, event, or experience might mean that you have to designate a time limit, after which you commit to focusing on other things.

Coping might involve admitting to yourself that despite your intentions and efforts, things did not turn out as you intended. You might think about how you may have contributed to the problem and determine how to respond differently if ever faced with a similar situation. Write down your resolutions in a private journal so that you can return to your notes if you need to. When feeling wronged, remind yourself that people do things according to their motives, not yours, and their intentions may not necessarily be what you perceive them to be. Remember that they are human too.

Rather than avoiding your feelings when something unexpected happens, try to understand the situation and recognize where you lack control. Teach yourself to let go by reminding yourself that you have already devoted a reasonable time to regretting the past and now you are ready to move forward. Give yourself permission to move past the obstacles and address any issues that you can solve that would impact your present and future.

Accept That Friends Will Come and Go from Your Life

The idea that friends will last forever is eloquently expressed in cards, mementos, and gift plaques. It certainly is comforting to think that certain relationships will last forever, and it is natural to hope that some do. At the same time, there will always be some that do not endure.

You need varying things from friendships at different points in your life. Experience constantly molds your thoughts, opinions, and perspectives. You mature and regress at different rates, depending on your reactions to certain events and the variety of things that you experience.

Some friends will come and go from your life just as you will move in and out of theirs. The most important aspirations to uphold are to never give up on someone you love and always try your absolute hardest to maintain family ties. When a friendship no longer satisfies, resist the urge to overanalyze or assign fault. Outgrowing a companion is not right or wrong. It is merely something that happens as you respond to your environment, learn, and change. Sometimes, you do what you need to do for emotional survival.

Moving to a different city, studying for a formal education, finding work experience, making new friendships, joining clubs, reading, traveling, and other activities expand and impact your personal outlook. These occurrences change your perceptions, what you enjoy, what you choose to pursue, and what you appreciate. It is only natural that some friendships fade while others, both old and new, flourish on different levels.

Forgive Yourself for Making Mistakes

Everyone makes mistakes. Why do you expect yourself to be different? Imperfection is a part of living. We all avoid tasks that we need to accomplish, forget people's names, and overlook special occasions. Sooner or later, we all do things we wish we had not done. We speak without thinking, procrastinate, find something difficult to learn, spill, get lost, boast, drink too much, eat as if we've never seen food before, criticize others, and more. If you have just read this list and could not agree with one thing, then you are probably lying and can forgive yourself for that!

Despite all efforts to avoid slip-ups, eventually both small and large errors are bound to creep in. Part of coping successfully with blunders comes from trying to learn from experience and improve your ability to manage adversity. Forgive yourself for making mistakes—you're only human!

Learn to Appreciate Yourself

It is easy to ignore the areas where you excel while encouraging others to develop their own talents. Learn to appreciate yourself by defining your aptitudes and skills. Write down everything you are good at, from untying knots to reading aloud.

Consider the activities that you are most drawn to and which ones come most naturally. Make an effort to raise your innate skills to new and higher levels—you will find it easier than trying to improve your abilities in areas where you lack natural interest or capacity. Effectively hone your talents by allotting the greatest percentage of your efforts toward practicing what you enjoy doing.

Appreciate each step of your progress. Success that involves overcoming obstacles is much more poignant than accomplishments that come easily. Nothing beats the feeling of knowing that the only reason why something important to you occurred is because you chose to pursue it.

Remember That Everything That Has a Beginning Has an End

Difficult periods appear endless when you are in the middle of them. When you feel as if trying to improve your mood and your situation are futile, remember that everything that begins also must end. Change is constant. You cannot and will not be in crisis or feel melancholy or stressed forever. Dwelling on the assumption that your unhappiness is permanent only contributes to the depth of your depression. When you feel disheartened, remind yourself that this too shall pass. Sunlight always follows darkness. Every day begins with fresh opportunities.

Cope with the Future by Understanding the Past

What experiences do you replay inside your head? Have you noticed that certain memories continue to surface, even years after the offence occurred? When you spot such patterns, choose to accept that some gaffes are going to impact your life and give yourself a pep talk to remind yourself that people make mistakes.

You deserve a present free from dwelling on shortcomings, blunders, or hurts from the past. Even if you have been wounded by unfair circumstances, use your power of free will to resist thinking, feeling, or acting like a victim. Try to understand the situation from the perspective of every person involved. Recognizing why things happen can help turn off the reruns inside your head and provide release from regrets, judgments, and "if only" thoughts that persist. Examine deep-rooted mindsets that may bias you and make a conscious choice to move forward. When understanding eludes you, work to accept what cannot be undone.

Unless you've invaded Earth from another universe, it is safe to assume that you are human, just like everyone else. Therefore, you too are going to slip up despite your best intentions. Accept that setbacks are one of the obstacles that make success even more powerful. Cope with the future by understanding the past, and appreciate your personal history as a series of experiences that contribute to your multi-faceted self.

Allow Yourself Time to Feel

In order to heal, you need to be in touch with your feelings. Crying is one aspect of emotion that allows you to express sorrow without formulating thoughts into sentences. Tears are a necessary means of responding to sadness, grief, and distress. According to some scientists, the act of crying allows the body to release abundant amounts of adrenaline and other stress-related chemicals. Shedding tension-relieving tears balances your body's stress levels and eliminates chemical build up, which restores harmony in your body's internal processes.

If you feel that your tears are uncontrollable (or are on their way to being so), try to manage crying jags by scheduling a time slot to focus only on what is upsetting you. Try for thirty minutes or an hour per day. If you need to cry during that period, do so—but outside of that allotment, try to put those upsetting thoughts aside. The experience will leave you feeling calmer, more refreshed, and better able to manage your day and your emotions.

Accept Your Disabilities

When you live with constant stress, depression, or anxiety, you live with a disability. Take heart in noting that other people find ways to work around emotional and physical difficulties—and you can too. While there are bound to be periods that are more wearying than others, there will also be days where your problems fade into the background.

Trust that the easier days will become more frequent. Rather than berating yourself when your feelings get in the way of accomplishing what you want to do, accept that your feelings result from an existing obstacle. Remind yourself that it is emotionally healthy to accept your anxiety as something with which you cope and use the skills you have learned to move forward and conquer what limits you.

Consider Whether Your Expectations Are Reasonable or Fair

Hope is the birthplace of your desires and one of the first steps to achieving satisfaction. However, certain aspirations can bring about an optimism that blurs into less productive feelings, such as that of entitlement. This is where, in the long run, dreams can mislead you.

Assess whether your expectations are reasonable or whether you are assuming that you deserve certain rights, perks, or rewards. Even when you feel as if your efforts should earn certain results, life does not guarantee meritocracy. "Should have" is a phrase destined to leave you frustrated.

Overcoming this stance means accepting certain truths. Life is unpredictable and constantly changing. Fairness is not guaranteed. Inconveniences are not reserved for others. Everyone has to wait, take turns, face obstacles, and experience failure. Some people will set their sights higher than yours, and others will aim for smaller goals. It takes hard work to accomplish ambitious endeavors. You—and only you—are responsible for making the effort required to reach your goals.

Learn to discern between practical and impractical expectations. Ask whether others would assess your contributions the same way you do. Are you under the impression that you deserve the things you want? Do you expect others to do more for you than you are willing to do for yourself? Note that you will never hear successful people credit their achievements to having maintained an attitude of self-entitlement. Those who succeed in gratifying their desires are more likely to persevere in reaching their expectations. They are further prone to view life's truths and circumstances as a means to make their dreams come true instead of complaining about how things "should have" been. Leave entitlement behind, and set your sights on healthy achievement.

Acknowledge Sorrow

While grieving is often associated with death, the emotion can be coupled with any loss. Financial ruin, failing health, an ended relationship, and numerous other traumas might trigger a time of mourning.

Whether you prefer to grieve privately or in a more open manner, there are going to be times when it is easier to pretend that you are coping. You might feel unable to endure people looking at you with pity or bear their stumbling words when they do not know what to say or how to help. You might feel as if you "should" have come to terms with your sorrow by a certain time. Unfortunately, it takes an enormous amount of energy to keep up appearances. That is why it is important to allow yourself to experience and express your feelings. Pick a time when you can either convey them in the company of people who understand how you feel or experience them alone when you can process what is upsetting you.

Help yourself cope by acknowledging your sorrow. You cannot resolve what is suppressed or ignored. Grief follows its own clock. Do not assign guilt-inducing timelines to your heartache. If people make remarks that inadvertently upset you, let them know that your feelings are your own and that judgement is not fair, helpful, or appropriate.

Exploring your pain will leave you better equipped to come to terms with the situation and maintain control in public situations. It will reduce the stress of insisting you are fine and the worry of falling apart at inopportune moments. No matter what kind of loss you have experienced, ease your emotional turmoil by first acknowledging that it is okay to be sad.

Conscientious Living

Define Your Dreams and Map How You Are Going to Achieve Them

What do you need to do to turn your dreams into real experiences? Effective planning will certainly be crucial. Seeking the best way to use your time is an intriguing challenge. Define where you are now, then outline where you would like to be in the major areas of your life in five year increments.

Consider relationship, career, educational, and recreational viewpoints. Now write down three steps that will move you closer to each goal. You are more likely to succeed if you keep track of your progress by reviewing your goals on a monthly basis. In order to make the changes necessary to keep up with unexpected occurrences, examine your list monthly and give it an annual overhaul every New Year's Day or birthday. If you do not stick to your plan, that's okay—goals can change and hobbies can lose their appeal. Actively defining possible activities, goals, hopes, and dreams helps you move away from distraction and closer to where you want to be.

Focus on Blue Skies Instead of Thunderclouds

It can be difficult to see beyond thunderclouds, but living with unsolved problems is easier if you focus on blue skies instead. When storms threaten your personal horizon, turn away from the rain to find the pleasing things that remain—the positives that brighten your day, the genuine people in your life, the acts of kindness that give you reason to hope. Even though stress and depression make it easier to feel cynical rather than optimistic, it is not impossible to adjust this dejection-inspired attitude. Consider these lines of poetry:

> "Two men look out from the same bars:
> One sees the mud, and one the stars."
> (Frederick Langbridge, *A Cluster of Quiet Thoughts*)

It takes a significant effort to turn your glance away from the mud and towards the sky, but the reward makes each attempt a trace easier. Instead of focusing on mistakes or missed opportunities, focus on the optimistic moments you experience. Instead of dwelling on what you do not feel capable of doing, highlight what you do achieve. Rather than surrendering yourself to a peevish attitude, use your knowledge, skill, and drive to center your energy where it will do the most good—keeping your eyes on the positive and looking for hope.

Even if you can only make a small effort, that is a significant and worthy accomplishment. Every attempt means that somewhere deep inside, you have faith that your situation will improve. Look for hope, celebrate your optimism, and enjoy the blue-sky moments.

Enjoy Your Own Story

Have you ever noticed your ability to forget the remarkable or carefree moments in your own life? You may not realize just how special you are. A great way to appreciate yourself is to make a list of fifty things that the people in your life do not know about you. Your list may include events, experiences, habits, dreams, jobs, promotions, relationships, awards, compliments, skills, or anything else that is special, important, or just surprising! You might include something humorous, such as the ability to yo-yo while skipping rope or the knack for fooling your family with an impersonation of Aunt Alma. Keep your list cheerful—this is your chance to show others (and yourself) how unique you really are.

You might also want to think about why these things on your list are private or not likely to come up in conversation. One fun test to see how well others know you is to ask a friend or family member to make a similar list and compare the two. This pleasant activity creates an opportunity to remember the things you like about yourself as well as to learn how others see you.

Look for the Reward When Something Bad Happens

A negative incident is easier to endure when you can learn something meaningful from the experience. The lesson may be blatantly clear or deeply hidden for years. It is most likely a message that would have been difficult to understand on its own.

Though a challenge to appreciate gifts shrouded in pain, it is worth searching for the wisdom when your internal peace or self-assurance are tested. Look for the reward when something bad happens. Practice steering your thoughts away from the hurt to focus on processing the information through prayer, meditation, conversation, journaling, or physical exercise until you find something worthwhile hidden in the bad. Motivate and comfort yourself with the belief that understanding and sharing your experiences and their lessons might help ease someone else's anguish.

Do a Kindness Every Day

Performing a daily kindness takes the focus away from you and your troubles and makes it easier to put your problems into perspective. The act of helping others builds self-appreciation and serves as an important reminder that you are not alone. Though some people's battles are clearly apparent and others more privately concealed, everyone experiences conflict at some point in their lives. Certain challenges are life-threatening, others are chronic, but everyone with worries benefits from the thoughtfulness of others.

Volunteering can be a rewarding way to be a part of something uplifting, but you do not necessarily have to give time to an outside organization to help others—charity begins at home. You could visit a bereaved relative, shovel snow off of a neighbor's sidewalk, give blood, or do anything else that makes you feel good and takes the focus away from yourself. Find ways to be compassionate towards others every day, and experience the benefits that boomerang back.

Exercise Your Brain

Scientists have shown that no matter your age, the more you think, the better your brain works. Mental stimulation improves cerebral function, so fight mental inactivity by striving to keep your mind working at peak performance.

You can accomplish this by challenging yourself with a variety of new and novel activities, especially those you have never done before. Studies show those who speak multiple languages, solve puzzles, read, or partake in other activities that demand mental effort protect themselves from cognitive decline.

Ensure that your mind functions at peak levels by undertaking actions as straightforward as changing routines: try doing things with your less dominant hand or take different routes when running errands. More involved activities also stimulate the brain. Play chess, take art lessons, study tai chi, learn to juggle, or travel. Try something new on a regular basis to exercise your brain and keep you operating at your best!

Consider Whether the Annoying Things People Do Really Matter

Born in 1873, Saint Thérèse of Lisieux was a Carmelite nun by the age of fifteen. She made a conscious decision to show God her devotion by enduring annoyances without protest, proving that no sacrifice is too small. She stopped herself from complaining about the petty frustrations caused by those around her. When repeatedly splashed with dirty wash water by an inconsiderate member of the order, Thérèse said nothing. When another made irritating noises during each prayer time, Thérèse remained silent. When wrongly accused of breaking a vase, this nun silently accepted the blame. Her writings stated, "The only way I can prove my love is by scattering flowers, and these flowers are every little sacrifice, every glance and word, and the doing of the least actions for love."

This virtuous behavior led Thérèse to be known as the "Little Flower." Now, you may think to yourself that even though she became a saint, you never will. It is easy to assume that these sacrifices came easy for Thérèse, but in fact she had a formidable temper as a child! Her first instinct was always to throw tantrums. Instead, Thérèse made an active decision to be different—and you can too. Consider whether the annoying things that people do really matter or whether you can disregard them.

Answer Your Social Conscience

Don't judge each day by the harvest you reap but the seeds you plant.
—Robert Louis Stevenson

The way you choose to live, the values you hold dear, and the causes you promote create the community and the world in which you live. When you hear yourself complaining about the ills of humankind, ask yourself who is supposed to solve the world's problems. In the end, change does not start at the top and work its way down; it starts with the individual who makes a difference for someone else. Activities that aid your community focus energy away from personal misery and achieve a win-win for everyone involved. Respond to community needs by taking an active interest in a charity or organization that works to improve society and lessen suffering.

Deliberately Refocus Your Thoughts

Control what images replay inside your head. One way you can accomplish this is by using self-distraction to consciously change your thoughts from negative to positive. Begin by preparing yourself with a mental list of some of your favorite memories or anything that brings a smile to your face.

The next time that you find yourself dwelling on a problem out of your control, change the subject to some of the positive points on your list. If you find yourself stuck, recite a nursery rhyme, poem, song, or multiplication table. Sing the alphabet backwards. Try to remember an elaborate joke from beginning to end. Any mnemonic exercise will work, as long as it requires your full mental capacity.

Give yourself time to make thought-refocusing a habit. With practice, this method will become a useful tool. Gradually, you will be able to focus your thoughts on the positive without drifting toward the negative in the first place.

Analyze Those You Admire

Ask a group of individuals to discuss whom they admire. Answers will span from historic figures to modern-day heroes, all known for their remarkable accomplishments. Depending on whom you ask, any field could be represented—from the arts to athletics, engineering, politics, or science. Insightful, intelligent, dedicated, courageous people have impacted and will always impact the world in noteworthy ways, and these endeavors are worthy of admiration.

However, sometimes a name will come up that is not famous. You may hear of everyday people who have overcome great difficulties. Someone may describe a friend or family member who bore an illness with dignity or fought social injustices. Someone may even be recognized as a loyal friend, a good listener, or a generous caregiver.

Consider those you admire and why they impress you. How can you build these traits into your own life based on your interests and goals? The effort will make you more satisfied with yourself—and may very well serve to inspire others.

Look for Positive Signs

Some days, you might feel surrounded by unhelpful people. You may have no patience for thorny personalities, distracted drivers, or abysmal service. Even though these inconveniences occur all of the time, it is best to delegate minor hassles to the place where they truly belong—your mental trash bin. If someone cuts you off in traffic, take a deep breath and forget about it. Accept back-handed compliments with grace and manage persnickety people like a born diplomat. Remember that no one escapes frustrations.

Rather than waiting for contentment to come your way, look for positive signs and change the outlook of your day. Focus on the little kindnesses that come your way—a stranger holding the door open for you, giving you a spot in line, or offering good directions. Appreciate the pleasure your senses bring—the smell of fresh cut grass, the call of a songbird, or the taste of fine chocolate. Peaceful feelings are more likely to occur when you pay attention and seek them out. Give yourself a well-deserved boost by disregarding all of the annoying things that pass your way and look for positive signs.

Apply Judgment before Offering Help

You probably wouldn't argue if you heard someone say that being nice is a good thing. Kindness is an important part of living a meaningful life. Ideally, caring actions create positive experiences for both the giver and receiver. However, sometimes people have differing ideas of where the limit of kindness should be. It is up to you to determine where your borders lie.

Compassion can be detrimental if it leaves you so busy trying to please others that you neglect your own needs or ignore other people whom you care about. Being nice is tied to maintaining self-esteem, but kindness that doesn't erupt from the heart is less likely to provide ongoing satisfaction. It may also come across as condescending or paternalistic.

Some people find it beneficial to share their frustrations with others. If someone comes to you looking for a conversation, use your best judgment to determine what they want to hear.

Note that not everyone's happiness depends upon your participation. Choose your giving and sacrifices with attentive judgment. Remember that most people voicing complaints just want to be heard and understood rather than helped or controlled.

Respond with Dignity

Almost everyone has stood speechless after someone directed a smart remark their way. Offering a suitable reply in the moment is a challenge when someone's words or behavior shocks you. Satisfying retorts that appear moments, hours, or even days later are frustrating but understandable. You want to respond in an appropriate manner, but it takes time to process every detail of a situation. Sometimes, you need to mull over the issue or take a breather before determining the best response. Rather than placing needless pressure on yourself to make spontaneous decisions, take some time before reacting to surprising situations and comments.

It is easier to brush off unkind treatment in a one-time situation. However, if a particular individual delivers put-downs on a consistent basis, you may need to undertake a less passive approach. If you choose to confront his or her verbal bullying, plan to do it in private. Refrain from raising your voice, making belittling statements, or using sarcasm. In a calm manner, simply state, "I'm trying to understand your attitude toward me. If I've done something to offend you, perhaps we can talk about it." Such a forthright approach may very well leave your antagonist speechless and embarrassed. Don't rush to fill an ensuing silence. Even if that person becomes defensive or in need of time to process a response, it is very probable he or she will think twice before needling you in the future.

Time always offers perspective. When days have passed and your temper has cooled, you might truly be thankful that you didn't give a rash or snappy comeback. The best way to inspire good behavior in others is to act with dignity.

Forgive Those Who Fail You

Consider this: you discover that you are destined to arrive at the pearly gates within a year. You inadvertently learn that you will receive a graph indicating the most grievous offences committed against you. Bars illustrate the instances when you forgave versus those when you held a grudge. The height of each bar indicates the amount of time you spent full of anger or resentment. What does your graph look like?

Reluctance to forgive is understandable. It comes from a natural reaction, an unwillingness to show kindness in response to people who hurt you. However, refusing to forgive is typically confused with agreeing to forget what happened. You may feel that by forgiving, you are allowing that person to get away with something unfair, and that is difficult to do, especially if you are still hurt. It is even harder if you see no indication of regret, sorrow, or distress.

There are reasons to forgive those who fail you. When you look back at how you spent your limited lifetime, you do not want to realize that you wasted precious moments on hostility, bitterness, or rage. Forgiveness does not ignore that something negative happened. It acknowledges the wrong and gives you control over your feelings, thoughts, and actions. Forgiveness resets your internal balance and keeps you thinking positive.

Practical Matters

Keep Fewer Dishes Rather Than Buying More Cupboards

Keeping fewer dishes rather than buying more cupboards takes discipline and a desire to focus on what is important in life. Organizing and purging your home of clutter means owning fewer belongings that require storage, dusting, polishing, and oiling—and thus, fewer things about which to think and worry. The end result is that you have more time available to pursue healthy, pleasant, and goal-achieving pastimes that bring genuine satisfaction as well as meaningful and beneficial personal growth. Pervading happiness is not achieved by shopping or owning things. Avoid letting your possessions own you. Sometimes the more you acquire, the less you enjoy what you already possess.

Define a Fair Level of Control

A sense of control is a great fuel for your confidence. You may feel more at ease when you command a situation because being in charge helps insulate you from the unexpected. However, you do not need to exercise power in certain situations to make up for a lack of it in other areas. Control that negatively impacts those around you is not ideal for you either. Examine whether your power-play is offending or alienating others. While strictly overseeing every situation possible may give you a sense of security and relief, it is wise to occasionally ponder and assess your motives.

Consider whether you obsess about controlling things that do not really matter in relation to your goals and other important aspects of your life. If you think that letting go is a weak reaction, try giving up control in situations in which the only consequence is positive for those around you. Relinquishing power can be as simple as letting your dining companion pick a restaurant for lunch. Exercising restraint could become your daily random act of kindness. Define a level of control that allows you to be both true to yourself and fair to others.

Tackle the Achievable

Some problems are more easily solved than others, so tackle simple dilemmas first. Working productively on manageable problems brings sustainable satisfaction and a rewarding sense of accomplishment.

Start by describing your stresses in specific terms. Rather than listing "I feel depressed," write "I feel down when my bank account dips below X dollars." Record possible solutions and the steps needed to reach preferred outcomes. Making a list helps focus on areas where you can do something constructive and provides a positive distraction from thinking about problems that are currently unsolvable.

After dealing with issues that you can solve, reexamine your more difficult matters. If they still feel insurmountable, commit yourself to working on one part of a single problem for fifteen minutes of every day. As you deal with your challenges in small increments, associated stresses will naturally diminish. You will likely find yourself working for longer periods as you feel progress occur. While not all problems are solvable, you can cope with your troubles more easily by aiming to tackle the achievable.

Anticipate Change

Whether anticipated with exhilaration or viewed with fear, change causes stress. While you cannot predict the future, you can try to anticipate likely situations and consider how to respond. This does not mean that you should look for the worst scenario that could occur and dwell on it. Nor does it imply viewing a situation with unwarranted optimism and assuming that all will work out for the best. It simply means taking the time to give a fair appraisal of all possible outcomes, reactions, and side-effects that could occur. Scrutinizing the impacts of potential change in a non-frantic manner serves you by ensuring an examination of possible responses in keeping with your personal goals.

Sort your thoughts by drawing a flow chart with "what if" scenarios, indicating the positive reactions or solutions. A thorough assessment reduces the unknown, calms nerves, and makes it easier to consider possible solutions to problems.

People around the world do this every day when they plan for retirement, life insurance, and funerals, all of which are inevitable eventualities. You can apply the same careful thought and preparation to other areas of your life by learning to anticipate change.

Reduce Stress through Physical Activity

When exercise moves in, depression moves out. While this may not come as a surprise, the benefits of physical activity on mood are great enough to justify a reminder. Take at least thirty minutes every day and do something invigorating to reduce stress.

If exercising is not one of your favorite pastimes, find ways to make it fun. Motivate yourself with a reward at the end of each session. Listen to music while you walk. Read a book or watch television while riding a stationary exercise bike. Go for ice cream after a swim—after all, this is about improving your mood, not losing pounds! If weight is a concern, choose a healthy treat that you truly enjoy, be it food-related or otherwise. Spending time with friends can be a beneficial incentive. Join a recreational sports league and do warm-up exercises and stretches on your off nights. Be creative! Go on hikes or walk down your favorite shopping street. Physical activity can take a multitude of forms and be different every day. It is not important how you do it as long as you are active on a daily basis.

Consider Whether You Talk about Something Too Often

There is a time for speech and a time for action. Become aware of when you do not contribute new information to a discussion. When you find yourself recycling the same story in conversation, examine why you gravitate to that particular vignette. Is there a certain aspect of a problem on which you tend to focus? You may need to examine whether you readdress certain experiences because some aspect has not yet been understood, resolved, or accepted. Consider whether you talk about something too much, and make up your mind to find a positive way to address the issue.

Use Adversity to Examine Priorities

Every adversity, every failure, every heartache carries with it the seed of an equal or greater benefit.
—Napoleon Hill

No one lives a life free of roadblocks, potholes, and detours. Sometimes, it just feels like the forces of conflict and confrontation gang up on you. While adversity is unavoidable, it does not have to be a meaningless struggle. You can use conflict to your advantage.

When faced with an unfavorable situation, look at similar struggles you have faced in the past, with and without success. How would you react to these situations today? Would you respond with instinct or a more intellectual approach? Do you think you would keep a cool head or be more inclined to panic?

Adversity is an opportunity to examine and set your priorities. Use it to focus your thoughts on how you want to spend your time and with whom you want to spend it. Consider it a catalyst, forcing you to sift through decisions, relationships, and activities that are immediately relevant versus those that won't matter by the end of the week. Time changes everything just as experience changes everyone.

Enjoy What You Can Control

Do you remember the days when you could not wait to grow up? As a child, you believe that you will be in control as soon as you have come of age. You will be able to make all of the important decisions in your life. Even as you relish the freedom, aging also brings awareness of the responsibilities associated with independence. You can choose to do what you like, but you will likely have to pay for your decisions financially and emotionally as well as offer up in return one limited commodity—time.

If your obligations become overwhelming, the idea of being in control may feel like a delusion. While some areas of life may be difficult or impossible to fully command, many are not. The reality is that while you cannot dictate your circumstances, you can control your beliefs, your words, and your actions. How you spend your time, with whom you share it, and where you spend it are all up to you. Make the effort to differentiate between what you can and cannot control, and focus on your spheres of influence.

Make a Business Plan for Life

Before starting a company, people create business plans to detail specific objectives, strategies, and responsibilities that the endeavor will entail. This sort of document forces you to think about resources, finances, competitors, and missing skills.

While it takes a lot of effort to create a business plan, the process is important because it forces you to consider each stage, from start-up to expansion and beyond. It is a roadmap that shows where you are, which way you want to go, and what you might face along the way.

Creating a business plan for your life can help you envision your ideal future. Chart your personal course by itemizing your strengths, examining any detrimental mindsets, and reviewing your financial situation. Make an inventory of the highlights; progress toward goals; obstacles you've overcome; and three-, five-, ten-, and twenty-year milestones you hope to achieve. List the skills you have and those you need to develop.

It can be inspiring to reflect on the past and nurture the present. Developing a long-term vision of your life stimulates hope. You may find that you have accomplished much more than you realize and feel increasingly motivated to persevere in your goals.

Support Yourself

Every struggle has unique qualities. In many cases, obstacles are easier to tackle and overcome in the company of others. Sometimes, meeting face-to-face is not possible. When you are unable to find anyone who shares at least some aspects of your experience, feelings of isolation can complicate your struggle.

If you crave human interaction and understanding, you might find it helpful to participate in an online support group of people coping with the same challenges. You can find such communities by entering a few descriptive words into a search engine and exploring what appears. Try "depression support groups" or any other combination of words. You may find it freeing to participate anonymously. If the first group you find does not feel like a good fit, look for another or start your own. A supportive, online community can take the edge off of feeling alone. In the end, you may even learn about local groups that meet in person.

However, sometimes face-to-face or online support systems are not available, and it is necessary to draw on your capacity to be self-supportive. Nurture yourself in the same way that you might care for a friend. Give yourself permission to indulge in small pleasures and build happy moments into your daily routine. When the need to talk to someone builds, try to release your feelings by writing in a journal, listening to music, or exercising. You might discover that self-support brings you the most solid sense of peace.

Prevent a Crisis

It's easy to justify postponing unpleasant tasks, conversations, and responsibilities. Perhaps you want to avoid a confrontation or you are optimistic that your problem will disappear.

Think of your concerns as dandelions. Without any attention, their roots reach farther into the Earth, and they multiply at an alarming rate. Just as dandelions persist, so will your troubles. The longer you neglect them, the larger they grow. It is up to you to take action and subdue them.

Stop procrastination by limiting your to-do list to your main priorities. Look at unpleasant undertakings in relation to how they fit with your goals. Sometimes, disagreeable situations need to be confronted head-on. If you need help making decisions, seek help. Try to make at least one effort to relieve your burden each day, and you will spare yourself a lot of discomfort. Prevent a crisis by tackling problems as they arise.

Put On Your Own Oxygen Mask First

Before an airplane takes off, safety instructions include the warning that in the event of decompression, an oxygen mask will drop from the ceiling and that you are to secure your mask before assisting those nearby.

On an airplane, you understand that you must initially take care of yourself so that you will be able to help others. Assisting your seatmate first would put both of you at risk. On terra firma, ignoring your needs in order to help someone else can be just as dangerous. Caring for others is important—however, you will be more effective in your endeavors if you reserve energy to attend to your own mental and physical needs first.

The next time that you decide to skip exercising, settle for an unhealthy meal, or give up sleep for someone else, be aware of the impact it will have on you. Sacrifices can be worthwhile, just be sure to make mindful decisions about what you choose to lose.

Refocus Your Attention

Just as a thought is born from experience, so are powerful emotions—they rise up and engulf you in an instant. These intense moments stem from memories and subconscious reactions that act as triggers—spoken words, painful questions, stitches on a quilt, wisps of a scent, or the opening notes of a song. Anything could send your mind careening back to a different time and place.

Unfortunately, strong emotions do not always present themselves at the most opportune times. Privacy is difficult to find in a public environment. While these sorts of emotions are hard to hold back, you can practice a few strategies to avoid embarrassing yourself. When you prefer to keep unwanted emotions at bay, limit their intensity and duration by refocusing your attention on your immediate surroundings. Force yourself to be in the present rather than stuck in your head. Try to notice something new around you, engage someone in conversation, read storefront signs—do whatever it takes to force your thoughts into the here and now.

Later, when you have privacy and the freedom to think without interruption, examine what caused your emotion. Try to view the situation as objectively as possible and in a detached manner, as if you are curious rather than emotionally invested. Eventually, you will find understanding and some level of acceptance. After a period of time, you may find that you have philosophized to the point that your interest diminishes along with the associated painful feelings, even when subsequent triggers occur.

Work to Develop Fulfilling Activities

How happy are you: somewhat happy, quite happy, or not happy at all? Do you feel a bit empty at the end of the day? Examine the elements in your life that contribute to (or detract from) your happiness and work to amplify the positives and subtract the negatives. Your life's undertakings should involve the types of challenges that grant fulfillment in the journey as well as the potential for success.

Look at the activities that already bring you pleasure. Perhaps you enjoy cooking. Enhance your skills by mastering a difficult recipe or by becoming an expert in a particular cuisine. If you like to write, experiment with a different genre or style. A gardener could try to grow a new rose hybrid. Try developing activities that bring you both enjoyment and a higher level of confidence—things that make you proud of your accomplishments.

Building on your current strengths provides a sense of purpose, a hearty distraction from worries, and perhaps even the thrill of discovery. Affirmation of a well-lived life comes from self-fulfillment. Focusing on what you can do rather than on what you cannot do is a positive method for achieving a sense of contentment.

Get Some Air

From a few weeks to six months, astronauts live in an unnatural environment. The International Space Station is an area that offers just a bit more room than a five-bedroom house. Astronauts in space experience long periods of time without being able to go outside to get some air. Some have said that the psychological challenges of living in a closed space and the inability to experience nature for extended periods of time are some of the most difficult aspects of working 220 miles above Earth.

First coined in 1918, the phrase "cabin fever" describes the bad tempered, restless feeling that occurs if you are stuck inside or feel isolated for an extended period of time. The irritability can range anywhere from slight to extreme.

You may not have a full-blown case of cabin fever, but if you are feeling crabby for any reason, boost your spirits by finding ways to breathe fresh air and enjoy some time in the outdoors. Visit a park, walk through a garden, and feel the sunshine—or rain or snow—on your face. Spending time in the sun gives the added benefit of a daily dose of vitamin D, which may help to improve your mood.

If something prevents you from getting outside daily, bring the outdoors in. Keep houseplants within your sight—even cacti do the trick. Buy fresh flowers, open windows, or install a skylight or roof window. You might consider opening your home to budgies, canaries, or other cheer-inspiring birds. Unless you're orbiting Earth, try to appreciate the outdoors and fit nature's mood-boosting qualities into your day.

Brainstorm for Possibilities

How many times have you expressed an idea only to hear someone call out "That's what I was going to say"? People considering the same information tend to suggest similar solutions when first trying to solve a problem. If it turns out your initial idea is not a viable possibility, enter into the fun world of brainstorming to introduce fresh thoughts and perspectives.

This process begins by clearly defining the issue to be solved. Rather than stating "I want 'something' to stop happening," you will find expressing a desired outcome to be more productive. Be as specific as possible, because it is easier to justify failure for vague goals. For example, "I want dinner guests to stop cancelling at the last minute" might become "I want Prestwick to find my meals too irresistible to miss." Restating this specific goal transforms it from a positive statement into a negative one, which also inspires more energy and excitement, because it creates an active situation that you can change.

Once you have clearly defined your goal, the next step is to suspend judgement until after you have finished listing as many ideas as possible. Working alone, you might set a quota of thirty ideas. If you have help, aim for seventy-five or one hundred. At this stage, no idea is too unworkable, bizarre, or complex. Make a rule that no one is allowed to halt the brainstorming process by discounting a suggestion.

Why is it useful to brainstorm? Because every suggestion—even the ridiculous ones—will lead to more ideas. Peculiar schemes can trigger workable solutions. Create an atmosphere free from judgement and your mind will open to new possibilities.

Know When to Seek Help

Suppose you could go to a salon and get treated with a new product that repels negative emotions. Once treated, every horrible feeling that typically takes hold of you slides off and away. There would be no side effects or stigma, and you would feel better.

If it were that easy to get rid of unhappiness, you would probably seek it out. But if you can see yourself choosing a miracle panacea, why can't you see yourself talking to a counsellor, therapist, psychologist, or psychiatrist? If you would hire a qualified individual to cut your hair, shingle your house, fix your car, put a cast on your arm, clean your teeth, teach your children, or care for your parents, why wouldn't you invest in someone who could help you process your feelings and develop optimal mental health?

Just as you may have to shop around to find the best person to cut your hair, you may need to do some work to find the right fit with a professional who can help bring your mind to a healthier place.

Remember that there is no shame in seeking help. If you find comfort in discussing your thoughts and experiences with others, then do not hesitate. Professionals are at your disposal to relieve your pain and build your mental strength. There is no reason not to invest in their knowledge. However, some people may negatively judge or discourage you because of their own stigma. You may not want to share your choices with those around you—and no one will force you to.

If you are not ready to follow this route for yourself, consider one more benefit. It will make you stronger for those who depend on you. If you believe that you do need someone else's help but feel worried or afraid, remember that the only side effect of getting help is feeling better.

Identity and Perception

Avoid Surrounding Yourself with People Who Continually and Deliberately Hurt You

Who has not felt the shock, dismay, and disappointment of being treated poorly, unfairly, or even cruelly? People who offer criticism instead of support, allow jealousy to dictate their responses to you, or otherwise hold you back should not be given the gift of your time. You have every right to insulate yourself from those who do not demonstrate respect for you. Remember that human dignity is a universal right. Whether by accident or intention, any person who repeatedly makes you feel bad is best avoided—especially when stress makes you vulnerable and susceptible to negative thinking.

If evasion is not possible, then consider discouraging negative interactions in a more direct manner. Try to talk through the issues with a close friend, but if that is not a possibility, seek creative solutions to reduce the longevity and frequency of unavoidable contacts. You might strategize to ensure that you are not seated together at gatherings or play loud, conversation-discouraging music. Avoid being alone together, and when dialogue is unavoidable, learn to control the conversation. Think of neutral topics in advance, and when necessary, change the subject.

If interactions with challenging people continue to arise, employ private humor! Tell yourself jokes. Rhyme the person's name with something that makes you smile, or (my favorite) keep an envelope of boring photos handy and make a habit of pulling them out for show and tell. Learn to wave the envelope invitingly and you will be the one who is avoided! The simplicity of storing photos in a smartphone makes this tactic even easier (and much more portable).

Have fun protecting your sanity and be proud to take creative actions to stop yourself from falling victim to another's lack of consideration. Your stress will be reduced just knowing you have coping options. You may enjoy a good laugh!

Overall, remember that despite the most admirable creative efforts, you can only control your own response to any situation. Avoid whom you must, and whenever possible take what is really the most positive action: surround yourself with people who have the maturity to accept and appreciate you for who you are. Spending time with positive people will make it easier to avoid dwelling on the negative interections that do arise.

Recognize That People Tend to Behave Poorly When They Feel Badly

You do not have to look far to find an irritable person. Why do people behave poorly when they feel badly? Because thinking of oneself before others is a human tendency. If you find yourself on the receiving end of out-of-line behavior, you are receiving the projection of someone else's pain. Remember that the hurtful incidents you experience can truly be unintentional. It is not always about you!

Look for this shortcoming in your own behavior. If you are guilty of using crankiness to express frustration, aim to resist the urge to conduct yourself in this manner. Strive to be patient when faced with daily vexations. An ill temper only creates more problems. The tendency to harp on other people is a habit you can realistically train out of yourself.

The next time that you feel inclined to complain, nurture solution-seeking habits instead. You will feel better about yourself and walk with greater pride when you master negative, purposeless impulses. If you remind yourself that people behave poorly when they feel badly, it will become easier to maintain a positive outlook as well as judge less harshly, overlook unpleasant situations, and forgive others who subject you to their moods.

Accept That Nobody Can Read Your Mind

Depending what's in your head at any given moment, it is both fortuitous and unfortunate that nobody knows how you feel except for yourself. Even you may struggle to define all of your emotions! At the same time, it feels great when you are exactly understood. If people could read your mind, you would be spared trying to explain your feelings and actions to others.

Since you are forced to choose what to disclose and what to keep private, it is vital to communicate clearly when you do decide to share. If you want understanding but no advice, say so. When you welcome an opinion, you may have to specifically ask for one.

If you do not get the reaction you anticipate or want, accept that it is often difficult for others to understand the people around them without having enjoyed or endured the same experiences—just as you cannot always appreciate someone else's enthusiasm or despair over different events. Rather than allowing yourself to make judgments, avert your frustration by choosing to shrug tactless or unhelpful comments away. Tell yourself, "No one can read my mind. Perhaps I can explain it more clearly next time."

Know That Failure Means You Are Trying

Success and failure are inherent results of human actions. A number of clichés sum up bits of time-honored wisdom on these topics: "You win some, you lose some;" "If at first you don't succeed, try, try again;" "Know when to quit." What these catch-all phrases imply is that the first time that you try something new, failure is a likely outcome, but that does not mean that you will never get it right. Setbacks and disappointments provide the experience and lessons you need in order to eventually master the challange—what is most important is that you continue to practice.

It is perfectly natural, normal, and expected that you will be proficient in some areas and not as skilled in others. Next time you fall short at some enterprise, be proud of the effort you have made. Trying your best is the most important and meaningful success of all. Persevere with pride, for failure means that you have the opportunity to grow and learn from your mistakes.

Ease Away from Destructive Self-Preoccupation

Do you think about yourself too much? Is such a thing even possible? Self-preoccupation is an important part of problem solving, but it can also overwhelm true priorities. Survival instincts require you to think about yourself and how to respond to your surroundings. You must plan your schedule and deal with any problems that arise on a daily basis. While self-preoccupation is an important part of problem solving, it is possible to think about yourself too much. In fact, it can overwhelm you enough to make focusing on your true priorities difficult. Be wary of engaging in disparaging internal chatter.

To best look out for yourself, reduce the amount of time devoted to self-fixation. Analyze your mental habits and consider whether too many of your thoughts are occupied with unproductive self-examination. Are you spending excessive time evaluating your actions, reliving long-ago events, or reviewing trivial conversations? Is your consciousness merely within your mind instead of with others around you?

Halting this mental static will enable you to focus on the present and perceive life from a more constructive viewpoint. Instead of second-guessing yourself, devote your consciousness to more meaningful concerns.

Use Gracious Thoughts to Nurture Peaceful Feelings

On a bad day, it is easy to feel as if every inconvenience, frustration, and disappointment is thrown your way. That driver cut you off on purpose. Your friend canceled dinner plans at the last minute. A client came late for an appointment and didn't call to let you know.

Before reacting to the negative moment, take time to consider the other person's perspective. Maybe that driver was rushing home to an injured child. Maybe your friend had a rough day at the office but wants to reschedule. Maybe your client had to pick up her kids early from school. The possibilities are endless, and as you are not a mind reader, try to understand the complete situation before blowing things out of proportion.

Your mood can change your entire day. Rather than letting emotional backlash determine your response to small inconveniences, set your default mood to one that nurtures compassion and understanding. Your bad days won't get worse and your good days will be even better. Spending fewer moments bemoaning inconveniences gives you more time to develop a good mood and healthy thoughts.

Embrace the Unpredictable

How much time do you spend thinking about the future? It's useful to ponder upcoming occasions, responsibilities that need to be executed, and the hopes you have for each. Anticipation helps you explore how to best prepare for upcoming demands. Despite the energy you devote to thinking ahead, life is unpredictable. It is impossible to guess how people will behave, what the weather will be, or how events will transpire. It is easy to get upset when your day does not go as planned.

When something unexpected happens, try to benefit from your frustration. It may be simple—an incredible sunset, a moment alone, a new appreciation for a friend. There may be a lesson to learn—how to better manage your time, be more selective about your relationships, or change certain habits. If the good in your situation is more elusive, it also may be more profound.

Some of the most satisfying experiences cannot be prearranged or predicted. Enjoy the benefits of spontaneity and embrace things as they happen.

Consider the Different Roles You Play

We often view ourselves in relation to our own roles and those of people around us: family member, spouse, girlfriend or boyfriend, caregiver, friend, neighbor, colleague, acquaintance. We also categorize by interests: occupation, hobbies, sports, and more. You are many things to many people, but who are you to yourself? Who do you want to be?

While you may spend significant hours accommodating responsibilities associated with each role, you also need time to fulfill your own needs. You can glean some of that time by making sure you incorporate the skills you use in different areas into your personal schedule. Consider the expertise that you bring to each role that you play and how you can transfer your skills across the various tasks you need to accomplish. For example, you may be very good at arranging your work day but lax in defining the same structure in your home obligations. If you apply your organizational skills to your home life, you ultimately will have more time to spend on yourself. Be aware of who you want to be and thoughtfully pursue those roles.

Remember that trying to fulfill too many responsibilities at one time can lead to slightly attending to everything but not actually achieving anything. Reassess and readjust your priorities and duties as new opportunities, experiences, and events impact your life.

Liberate Your Thinking

If you have ever chastised yourself for making the same mistake more than once, you are not alone. Everyone experiences the infuriating feeling of relearning lessons they thought they already knew. Before you kick yourself too hard, accept that frustration is tied to growth. Reassure yourself that imperfection is not the same as inadequacy. Mistakes, oversights, and failures do not make you unlovable or unworthy. Your flaws are an integral part of what connects you with others.

Everyone shares the experience of relearning some of life's lessons. Despite other people's advice, certain things have to be tried and realized for yourself. Hearty optimism may lead you to retry actions that have previously failed. Courage may egg you on. Never denigrate yourself for trying, even if it means that you discover something that you already knew. Liberate your thinking to embrace the idea that trying your best is more rewarding than trying to be perfect.

Imagine How You Would Help Someone with the Same Problem

It is always more challenging to make problem-solving decisions for yourself than it is to help others with their problems. Everyone else's difficulties seem less complicated—perhaps because it is easier for people to think with a clear head and retain objectivity when not personally invested in an outcome.

The next time you're faced with making a difficult choice, staving off trouble, or managing a crisis, imagine that the situation is happening to someone else. Think about the guidance you would provide if this person were faced with your exact circumstances. Would you be more likely to recommend compromise or steadfastness? Verbalizing the anger or keeping it quiet? Expressing optimism or abandoning the cause?

Try looking at your own dilemmas from an outside perspective. Visualizing how you would help someone with the same problem can help you to clarify your own paths to resolution.

Pay Attention to Recurring Messages

People generally behave in ways that are in tune with their own values, desires, and beliefs. Sometimes, however, people change, and the way they feel or act may differ from what used to be familiar. It can be a challenge to understand when people move in a different direction. They may send you subtle signals or messages in words or body language, so try to pay attention if someone acts in a manner that you consider strange. When people are up-front, take them seriously.

Imagine someone saying to you: "I don't value our relationship as much as you want me to. My needs will always come before yours. I'm not motivated enough to make sacrifices for you." Would you take notice? Most likely. However, few people will express themselves in such a forthright manner. To be so blatant would be terrifying, both for the speaker and the listener.

Reading a relationship means being attentive to the consistent messages behavior reveals. When exchanges are open, relationships grow more smoothly. As circumstances change, you may need to seek understanding through honest conversation. Allow for communication mistakes and setbacks on both sides, but pay attention to recurring messages. They are consistent for a reason.

Choose Your Orbit

In one day, our entire planet completes a full rotation. In one month, the Moon circles the Earth. In one year, the Earth completes its orbit around the Sun. Though the path you take cannot be predicted like those of the celestial bodies, you do get to select your direction.

The problem is that you may not always grasp which way to go. Perhaps you have a subconscious awareness but have not asked the right questions to move in that direction. When you reach a personal crossroads with no map in sight, ask yourself what it would take to overcome your reluctance. Question how your values weigh into this decision and rely on past experiences to guide you. Perhaps it is most important to consider what will happen if you do not act.

There are many questions to ask. Each one brings to light fresh considerations that can impact your future. Questioning the unknown is an infinite process to which there is no final solution. So, rather than being swept along a path you did not select, choose your orbit today.

Distinguish between Dreams to Pursue and Dreams to Enjoy in Thought

We dream constantly: while running errands, while waiting in line, while sleeping. Some dreams recharge our brains and analyze things that happen during the day; others present fairytales that seem too good to be true, exploring our most alluring desires. Have you ever berated yourself for not making a dream become reality? Perhaps you regret not trying hard enough to solidify a particular vision into something more concrete. Life could be so exciting if only you had more courage, more perseverance, or more talent.

Don't despair! There are good reasons for dreaming the unachievable. Dreams about whom you could be, what you might do, or where you should go allow you to explore ideas, understand strengths, tackle weaknesses, and determine where your true passions lie. Just as brainstorming leads you from unworkable (and sometimes crazy) ideas to genuine inspiration, dreaming takes you from unrealistic whims to desires you can achieve. Daydreaming allows you to invent new, tangible possibilities. Plans that lead you to something exciting very often result from such dreams.

Allow yourself to indulge in fantasy, but remember that not every wish needs to come to fruition for you to be successful or happy. Distinguishing which dreams to pursue and which to simply enjoy will allow you to reach your fullest potential.

Appreciate Your Individuality

Have you ever noticed that every popped kernel of corn erupts into a different shape? Though each one is unique (and delicious), it is unreasonable to grade one piece of popcorn as more special or important than another. There would be no purpose in declaring one to be the best kernel and labelling the others as the worse kernels.

It is equally nonsensical and unproductive to spend your time trying to rate yourself better or worse than other people. While acting on competitive desires contributes to having purpose, remember that uniqueness is about distinctiveness and not quality. Abilities and interests naturally evolve and fluctuate over time. Regardless of your circumstances, you do not lose or gain value as a person as the years go by.

In order to appreciate your inimitable self, you need to like who you are rather than just what you are capable of doing. Appreciate your individuality. Rather than expending energy to outdo others, devote your drive to creating new personal bests. Work on being the best individual you can be—no one can compete with that.

Choose Which Experiences Define You

Governments characterize countries, products distinguish manufacturers, and physical traits identify animal breeds, but what defines you? Consider the overriding elements that drive your thoughts, motivate your decisions, and trigger your behaviors. Do you focus on past events or present circumstances? How do your beliefs and values determine your actions? Do you define yourself through your abilities, shortcomings, or dreams?

Think about your specific qualities. Remember moments that have stayed with you over the years. Look beyond your job title, relationships, and credentials. Examine who you are rather than the roles you hold. Your worth is the result of your humanity, not your achievements or failures. If you suffer from low or damaged self-esteem, ask yourself whether you are going to let your true essence dictate your sense of self or whether you mean to give that power to other people and their opinions. Remember that you matter.

Once you recognize the influences on your self-defining thoughts, challenge negative thinking and redefine your self-image. How you choose to characterize yourself will depend on your interpretation of life's events, not the circumstances themselves. Do not be afraid to incorporate the good and the bad. Rather than succumb to emotional triggers, look at each experience in both positive and negative terms. On what do you pride yourself? What could you have done differently? Altering your perspective may not be an easy task, but the effort will provide results. Examine your past and determine who you are and who you want to become.

Live in Reality

In a book I read during my childhood, a young girl is intrigued by a sagging, creaky-looking house in her neighborhood. She was warned never to go up the sidewalk and forbidden from entering the yard, even on Halloween. Instead, the girl invented fanciful stories about the crusty woman who lived there and the secrets the house held. While passing by one blustery day, the girl decided that even if she was absolutely certain it was safe, she would not go in. The truth would ruin what her imagination had created.

Even though I read this book as a child, I still find it remarkable that the character—even when consumed with curiosity—chose fantasy over fact. I still wonder whether there are times when it's better not to know the truth. Is it ever appropriate to choose a fiction over a reality?

At times, it may seem safer to live in your imagination. But the easiest and safest routes are sometimes the least satisfying of all. While sad truths can disappoint and cause great pain, a life filled with their sadness is infinitely more desirable than living a life based on fallacies. Rather than succumbing to the whims of your imagination, make your life meaningful by facing facts.

Be Aware of Your Points of Influence

Every day involves making judgments based on your sensitivity to what you perceive as right or wrong. But do you know yourself well enough to define your points of influence? To what extent do religious beliefs, moral standards, rules of conduct, and professional ethics guide you? How do education, media, and society's norms play a role in the values with which you associate? Is your reasoning based solely on personal experience, or do you favor a more universal perspective? How much weight do you assign to the opinions of family, friends, colleagues, acquaintances, and strangers?

It is useful to identify what values you hold most dear and from where they developed. Examine why they matter to you and how your outlook has evolved as you have grown older and accumulated more experiences. As a result, you have gained a position of knowledge and awareness that makes it easier to respond to moral dilemmas in ways that are consistent with your beliefs. Be aware of your points of influence, and your principles will guide you.

Meaningful Days

Do Not Schedule Every Minute of Your Time

Have you ever felt that even the smallest things seem to take longer than they should? Even if you are a master scheduler, planning every moment of your time only is going to leave you frustrated and uninspired. Creativity, a trait you naturally apply to all problem solving situations, cannot flourish and replenish without a mental holiday. You need time to day dream and to just "be" without having to justify your activities to another person or to yourself.

Creativity is important to happiness because it nurtures the elements that make you a unique individual. It enables you to look at situations from different perspectives in a non-judgmental fashion. Creativity feeds free thought, allowing you to think spontaneously and without fear.

Ease the pain of feeling frustrated, down, and depressed by avoiding scheduling every minute of your day. Instead, give yourself time for unstructured, unrestricted, and undemanding reflection—the natural solution for creative problem solving.

Accumulate Meaningful Experiences

Make memories to keep in your heart by accumulating meaningful experiences. It is your responsibility to ensure that the choices you make on how to spend your time result in recollections worth treasuring.

Is it more important to have a dandelion-free lawn or a child who believes that he or she is important to you? Would you prefer to one day dwell on your well-organized garage or reflect on time spent with a friend in need, impressionable teenager, or retired parent?

Rather than leave time to chance, think about what you can do today to avoid guilt or regret when you look back upon the years of your life. Choose to live wisely by making memories worth cherishing.

Give Worries the Day Off

Good news! No rule states that you must worry every day. In Margaret Mitchell's *Gone with the Wind*, Scarlett O'Hara thwarted love, the Civil War, death, poverty, snobbery, and countless other struggles. She helped herself remain calm through her troubles by repeating the mantra "I'll think about that tomorrow."

It is hard to accept that some problems cannot be solved to complete satisfaction. You may feel compelled to try again and again with different approaches and fresh possibilities. Putting worry on hold does not mean that you get to avoid problems forever, but it does mean that you give yourself a vacation from stress. The very postponement of worry can be liberating. You may gain a valuable perspective by taking a holiday from the emotion attached to anxiety. An unexpected eureka solution may surface. Give yourself an hour, a day, a week. Any and every amount of time you manage to divert is a healthy retreat. In between breaks, if your worries start to overwhelm you, repeat your own mantra to get you through the day.

Nurture Your Sense of Humor

Good-natured laughter is one of the best contagious things in life. As well as helping to alleviate stress, depression, and pain, it provides positive connections with others and makes it easier to consider situations from varying viewpoints. Medical research indicates that laughter may even improve certain medical conditions.

One of the reasons that a case of the giggles makes you feel good is because it forces your mind into the present moment. You can't worry and laugh at the same time. Best of all, you can enjoy it without limits—no overdoses have ever been reported.

While hilarity is typically spontaneous, you can still nurture your sense of humor. Spend time with fun-loving people. Visit the humor section of a bookstore, borrow comedy DVDs from the library, or download funny podcasts to your computer. Fill a folder with witty jokes, silly photos, and newspaper comics. Find ways to incorporate pastimes that trigger laughter into your daily routine. Consider watching stand-up comedians and improvisation artists as well as comedy television. Read jokes and limericks and play the type of board games that get you giggling.

Make a list of your most hilarious memories and reread it when you're feeling down. You might even practice telling funny stories so that you are prepared to share them with others. Spend time with those who embrace hilarity. Look for people who like to have fun and see the humor in their own lives. Surround yourself with others who laugh. It is refreshing to focus on carefree thoughts and forget yourself in happy-go-lucky merriment. Most importantly, learn to take yourself less seriously and see the humor in your own life. Try to devote at least a few minutes to good-natured laughter every day.

Do Not Waste Time Trying to Win Over Those Who Do Not Want You for a Friend

Life has a finite amount of time. Would you rather be with those who appreciate you or spend time trying to convince people to like you? Without giving up your right to be treated with respect or your obligation to treat others courteously, it is emotionally healthy to remind yourself that it is not necessary for every person in the world to like you.

Disinterest and even dislike are not necessarily personal. Feelings are often based on intangibles over which you have no control. Forget about winning over every person you meet and focus on embracing those who actively want to be with you.

Give Your Nights to the Sandman

An achievable and vital part of superior mental and physical health involves getting enough sleep. Decent rest enables you to better cope with stress, spend time in productive ways, and make rational decisions. While a well-rested brain improves emotional and social functions, sleep deprivation can cause you to experience memory impairment, poor physical performance, difficulty concentrating, and irritability.

Sleep is said to enable the human nervous system to function at its best by resting the parts of the brain that control social interaction and emotion. Scientists theorize that sleep allows the brain time to repair neurons, replace chemicals, and exercise important neuronal connections that might otherwise deteriorate from lack of activity. Sleep may allow the brain time to reorganize data to help solve problems, process new information, and sort and archive memories. When the body is asleep, the brain has a chance to rejuvenate.

Do not let the simplicity of getting adequate sleep undermine its importance. If stress is making it difficult to fall or stay asleep, give yourself a buffer zone to allow your brain time to wind down so that sleep comes more easily. Two hours of relaxation before bedtime is ideal. Avoid activities such as running errands, housework, or phone conversations. For the last hour, read or listen to music rather than watch television or use devices with a screen, as the light can over-stimulate your brain. Also, try to set up a consistent sleep schedule so that your body can begin to anticipate when it needs to wind down. Aim to relax and prepare for lights-out within two hours of the night before. If you want your days to run more smoothly, give your nights to the sandman.

Do Something for Yourself Every Day

As a gentle and consistent reminder that you are a deserving individual, make sure that each day contains something special just for you. Try to choose an activity in which you would not typically engage. Your ideal choice also will have a positive aspect, such as taking forty-five minutes to read, walk, or devote to some neglected hobby. That's right—deciding to try a new kind of doughnut each day is not the answer. Fill in your family tree, take a course in astronomy, or train a pet. Choose a pastime that does not rely on anyone else's presence or involvement.

Respect your need for personal time and consider it an entitlement. Exercising your right is a subtle, effective way to nudge your spirits a notch higher. If you feel like you're struggling to find time to devote to what brings you happiness, look at how you typically spend your twenty-four hours. Pay particular attention to the amount of time that you devote to activities that are not meaningful. You do not want to look back at your life and realize the number of hours spent on pursuits that provided no enrichment, such as watching reruns of television shows or poking people on Facebook. Reclaim your day! Your job is to make time for activities that encourage a healthy mental state and make your life more fulfilling.

On the inevitable occasions when you lack motivation to turn away from electronics, remind yourself how good you typically feel after treating yourself well. Because this new habit is intended to encourage your self-honor, do not berate yourself when you miss a day. Pick an activity that you truly like rather than something you think you ought to do, and the day will be yours for the taking.

Question the Routines in Your Life

You control your own destiny. Ask yourself whether you might enjoy life more if you spent a portion of your time differently. Exert your free will to choose pastimes that provide a positive distraction from troubles. Read up on new perspectives; nurture an acquaintance into a friendship; take an unusual holiday; sign up for a class in which you would not ordinarily participate.

Shake up your habits and schedule. Change your seats at the kitchen table or start new holiday traditions. Have dinner at an ethnic restaurant that offers unfamiliar dishes. Walk the dog through an unfamiliar neighborhood. Read a different newspaper. Shop at a new mall or go into unusual stores. Relive activities from your childhood: tossing a football, picnicking in the park, reading in a hammock, or collecting rocks. See what enjoyable activities you can reincorporate into your life.

Integrate anything that makes the present and future more cheery and helps to reduce triggers associated with unpleasant memories. Questioning the routines in your life can pull you out of a rut and provide positive distractions from daily lows.

Make Lists and Start Small

It is harder to succumb to stress and depression when you are distracted. Make a list of daily and weekly tasks that you can complete realistically. Focus on reaching small goals to reduce the number of minor but worrisome responsibilities that build up during the day. Writing items down and subsequently checking them off reduces the clutter of pending errands and anxiety that accompanies waning spirits. It allows you to know exactly what you need to do and what you have already done without having to think about it.

If the length of your list zaps your motivation, reward yourself when you finish a task. For example, after fifteen minutes of filing old bills, read one chapter of a novel. This will give you a sense of control and accomplishment, as well as a welcome break from bigger problems. Making lists and starting small puts you in a better place to deal with more challenging responsibilities.

Give Yourself the Gift of Time

True emotional health demands a certain amount of personal time spent in mental reflection. Rejuvenate yourself and ease daily stressors by saving a few quiet moments for yourself. Make your downtime a commitment so that you can revel in being alone—those minutes or hours belong to no one else. Use the pause to ponder positives, organize thoughts, or appreciate the good. If you are a religious person, you may find it beneficial to pray. Find the oasis in your mind by nurturing yourself each day with the simple gift of time.

Use Setbacks to Your Advantage

Imagine a simple problem—trying to open a pickle jar with a lid that is too tight. Your first attempts to open the jar are methods that have worked in the past. You run the jar under hot water, bang the lid with a heavy can opener, or use a rubber grip to turn the top. Nothing works, and it is driving you crazy! You really want to eat that pickle.

When you face a problem but find your progress stalled, view impediments as setbacks rather than defeats. Obstacles force you to seek resourceful solutions and often lead to better results than initial plans could yield.

Begin by managing your frustrations. Disappointment, aggravation, and exasperation have value. Each is a driving force for new ideas. You might combine past efforts to create a stronger effect. Hold the jar underwater and tap the lid against the faucet, or ask someone to grasp the lid with the rubber grip while you twist the bottom. You might seek a pair of stronger hands. Some schemes will not work; others will create new problems instead. For example, taking a hammer to the jar, although creative, is not safe, as broken glass is dangerous.

Don't give up. While overcoming an obstacle can be a trying matter, your true advantage lies in the effort you make. Using creativity to overcome setbacks generates satisfaction. If you start slowly, managing larger problems with greater ease will become a matter of habit.

Build Anticipation into Your Life

When you have trouble putting down a book, walking away from someone telling a story, or turning off a movie, it is because the suspense of the unknown has captivated you. You have become increasingly curious—filled with expectation of what is going to happen next. It becomes important to find out whether you have made an accurate prediction or whether you will find yourself surprised.

Anticipation is a delicious feeling. In stories, it brings delight. In real life, it builds purpose, nurtures hope, and creates optimism. Incorporating activities that you look forward to in your life makes tough times easier to bear. When you're feeling down, planning exciting activities can help transform you from bystander to participant. Anticipation also makes it easier to tolerate frustrations, cope with displeasure, and complete mundane tasks.

Invest time in contemplating what activities and events motivate you. Which ones make you feel like getting up early to start or staying up late to finish? Once you identify a few ideal pastimes or special events, plan, prepare, attend, and savor each experience. Commit them to memory—fun times last longer that way.

Keep Yourself Occupied

When faced with obstacles or confrontations, your body is chemically designed to make an instinctive, decisive response—fight or flight. Sometimes, neither option is successful. Lashing out may not make a difference, and retreating might make you feel powerless and vulnerable. When this happens, the only option left is to wait. Remaining optimistic when you reach an impasse is not easy. It is frustrating to feel helpless, waiting in hopes that one day your situation will improve due to events beyond your control.

Two situations can make a wait endless. The first is when you have no idea how long you must wait, and the second is when you must endure it alone. One of the best ways to ease the passage of time is by staying occupied and enjoying the company of others. Activity and conversation will distract you from your troubles, while immobility and solitude can make it much easier to dwell on frustration, sadness, and helplessness.

Note the times when your mind typically dwells on unhappy circumstances. If you find that your despair grows when daily circumstances demand patience, plan ahead by keeping distractions handy. Find activities to keep your mind engaged, such as a book, crossword puzzle, or game to prevent your thoughts from focusing on your anxiety. Listen to music, do some stretches, or reorganize your closet. Temporary diversions can make frequent waits seem much shorter.

Celebrate Progress As Much As Achievement

Imagine what life would be like if there was a universal rule that you must succeed before you celebrate. You would never be able to cheer during a promising home-run, applaud mid-performance at a concert, or offer a toddler a high-five for a first step after falling down.

It is important to celebrate progress, not just performance. Taking time to appreciate and acknowledge your growth encourages you to refocus on your goal and maintain—or increase—momentum. It is easier to persevere when reaching noteworthy milestones brings you pleasure. Finding ways to enjoy the process of achievement can bring the final victory closer to you. If your efforts are not only about the end results but also about advancement, you will be more satisfied about your final accomplishment, even if it is not realized in the way you anticipated. Achievement is typically the result of numerous incremental steps, so energize yourself along the way by celebrating progress as much as the desired end. Sometimes, you may even find that the journey is worth more to you than the completed goal.

Clear Communication

Define Your Feelings with the Right Words

Using the right words to define your emotions helps you better understand your state of mind. Develop emotional accuracy and honesty by choosing specific words over general expressions. This will enable you to clarify where your true frustrations lie. Knowing how you really feel will make it easier to accept and solve problems in healthy ways.

Can you differentiate between being angry and feeling neglected? Are you claiming to be "just tired" or are you in fact irritable because you are lonely? Suppose a friend whom you are supposed to meet arrives well past the agreed time. Instead of expressing yourself with a vague statement such as "I'm so upset," try to describe the source of the feeling by saying, "I don't feel respected when people keep me waiting."

Once you learn to define your emotions and their triggers, ask yourself if your response is realistic. What other reasons could someone have for being late? If you truly discern a lack of respect, why do you think they have this perspective? What is the best response and what can you learn from this situation?

Properly naming emotions will lead you from making general complaints to defining difficulties that can be addressed. It is a lot easier to find solutions when you can accurately pinpoint obstacles.

Defining and understanding positive emotions is also an advantage. If you believe shopping makes you happy, try to think in more specific terms. Suppose you describe the shopping experience by saying, "I like going to the mall because there are always people around. I enjoy chatting with sales clerks." Now you can understand that it is not the mall, the stores, or the purchases that are important. It is the people. How might you satisfy your natural need to interact with others?

Practice the Art of Conversation

Developing the art of conversation is a practical way to challenge yourself to expand your communication skills. Good conversation involves speaking with sincerity and listening with genuine interest. Conversing in ways that put others at ease enables you to replace stereotypes with new perspectives by learning more about the people with whom you speak. Of course, you may have your impressions confirmed, but you won't know that unless you make the effort. Either way, you can improve your understanding of human nature by discovering the many different motivations people have for their behaviors. The byproduct is a greater acceptance of the shortcomings of others—especially of the behaviors that aggravate you.

Imagine thinking that you have been ignored, only to discover that the accused rarely talks because of embarrassment over an accent. Suppose you feel critical of someone that slighted you. What if, despite the provocation, you were to engage that person in conversation and discover that she or he is stressed from lack of sleep while caring for a sick child? It is easier to forgive and overlook frustrations when aware of another's problems.

Positive relationships are founded on strong communication, which includes sharing ideas, experiences, and perspectives. Making an effort to engage in good conversation enhances human interaction. Developing a feel for what works and what does not will enrich your life, provide positive distraction, bring joy to someone's day, and allow you a temporary but important diversion from stress. Work to make these distractions happen more frequently. Practicing the art of conversation may also spare you a certain amount of boredom and reduce any feelings of loneliness.

Choose Success over Revenge

When hurt or angry, your first impulse may be to shout, "Someone's going to pay for this!" When you feel the need to share the pain, remember that your time is too valuable to waste on being vindictive. Turn anger's energy into a fuel that propels you to new, constructive actions. Use sadness to build your determination to grow.

When you look back on your hours, days, weeks, and years, you want to know that you did not squander a precious moment by trying to get revenge for something petty. Vindictive behavior ultimately leaves a shameful feeling, while rising above your frustration gives automatic (personal) bragging rights. Use your time wisely so that you feel good about yourself. True success lies in enjoying your life, and personal success is the best revenge that you could ever concoct.

Take Risks to Grow

It is hard to move forward when seemingly insurmountable obstacles leave you feeling wounded and vulnerable. Although wronged or worried, it is important to remember that you do not have to support a victim mentality. Do not let feelings of resentment turn helplessness into an acceptable state. Leave your comfort zone by facing any risks that you feel prevent you from reaching a better place. If you know where to look, you can find encouragement even in the midst of disappointment, rejection, and defeat. Heartening thoughts often begin with "Well, at least . . ." You might find yourself saying, "Well, at least no one was hurt," "Well, at least you tried," or "Well, at least you know not to do that again!"

When you experience disappointment, face your frustration by examining the situation to find a positive thought or lesson. On occasion, the message is exceedingly apparent, while at other times you may be perplexed for much longer. No matter how lengthy a period you need to invest, improving your peace of mind is a responsibility that you have to yourself. The result will be a foundation of inner strength that helps you to recognize new opportunities to leave pain behind and grow.

Define Your Motivations

Have you defined what you want, outlined steps to reach your goals, but still struggled to achieve? You may be finding that the end result is not rewarding enough to inspire a dedicated effort. Don't waste time rebuking yourself for a lack of self-discipline. The factors that make a person feel committed to a deed are very individual. What triggers one person to action may hold no satisfaction for another.

Consider intrinsic benefits, such as whether or not you will enjoy the process, maintain your values, and achieve personal satisfaction or pleasure along the way or from the end result. Examine extrinsic rewards such as prestige, recognition, or financial gain. Defining what drives you will enable you to build your goals around the stimulants that get you most excited and passionate. Make achievement a meaningful and successful process by harnessing the powerful force of your individual motivations.

Incorporate Genuine Compliments into Communication

It feels great when people give you compliments. Think of what you like and appreciate in the people around you, and then find ways to tell them. Incorporating genuine compliments into your conversations helps you to develop and practice the habit of looking for the good in others as well as focusing thoughts away from your own stresses.

The best accolades help people see themselves in new ways. Give praise that is specific rather than general. Try exclaiming, "I love the way you add accessories to make a look your own" instead of merely saying, "You look nice." Replace "Good job" with "You have a knack for taking a complicated problem and figuring out the best way to handle it."

Consider offering genuine and appropriate praise to people you do not find especially endearing, and watch those relationships become a little less trying. People are less likely to criticize your ideas and opinions when you state truths that make them feel good—in fact, they will be more willing to offer you genuine compliments in return! Incorporating good will into your communication benefits everyone involved.

Define What Success Means to You

Examples of extraordinary achievement, accomplishment, and victory are everywhere. A scientist makes a notable breakthrough in diabetes research. An athlete sets a world record. A legless man climbs a mountain. Seemingly impossible goals are reached every day, and agendas are set to a higher standard. When those around you voice their opinions about how success is qualified, remember that in the end it is defined by individual perception—and each viewpoint will vary.

Without realizing it, the bombardment of others' impressions causes self-judgment, and some of these opinions come from agenda-ridden media sources or people whom you don't even know! You may feel pressure to conform to what others believe, but remember that some people seek conformity as a means to validate their own opinions and self-worth.

While it is important to acknowledge the efforts and viewpoints of others, defining your success means adhereing to your own standards. What is most meaningful to you? What level of accolades is necessary to sustain your pride? What reveals the most genuine form of satisfaction? Find, establish, and pursue your own measures. When you reflect on your life, you will be satisfied because you aimed for the most worthwhile goals.

Give Up the Need to Be Right

Isn't it nice to be right? Having all of the answers can amplify your confidence. The trick to sharing your knowledge lies in making sure it doesn't blur into showing off your smarts or forcing your opinion where it's not wanted.

Listening to those who are right (and those who insist they are right) can be tiresome. Enrich your conversations and your relationships by discerning when a debate is a wise choice. Give others the opportunity to share their knowledge—they have had different experiences and have learned different things. Accept that other people do not think like you. Ask yourself whether the point you feel compelled to make is worth pursuing. What is the value in forcing your truths on others? At times, there may be no value whatsoever.

When you disagree with others, consider their perspectives. Remember that people who feel heard are more likely to be receptive to your words. You do not need to abandon who you are and what you believe in order to listen to someone else's point of view. Appreciate what everyone brings to the discussion and conversations will remain peaceful rather than competetive. People will find speaking with you to be a richer and more meaningful experience.

Record Your Personal Stories

People have told stories since the beginning of time. Storytellers practice their art for pure pleasure as well as to impart wisdom, share history, and preserve culture. Stories make people laugh, feel connected, and explore a range of emotions.

Everyone has tales worth telling. Recording your personal experiences is a healthy self-reminder to laugh at yourself and with others as well as a way to celebrate life. Being able to reflect is also a way of healing—your perspective about an experience at age ten may not be the same as your outlook at twenty, fifty, or seventy.

Think about your life in chronological order and list your own compelling stories. Some may be very short; others may fill pages. What is your earliest memory? Did you ever break a bone or have to go to the hospital? When were you most frightened? Do you remember things that made you laugh or feel embarassed? What are the stories that people ask you to retell?

Record your memories however you feel most comfortable. Some may have dialogue, full scenes, and a snappy ending, while others may just be a list of phrases that trigger your memory. Over time, conversations you have, books you read, music you hear, or other experiences will bring back more memories to record.

Use your stories to appreciate your unique life. You will see how far you have come and the value of your many experiences along the way.

Nurture Creative Thinking

The word "creativity" often brings artistic skills to mind, but the potential to express and use what lives in the imagination extends well beyond the arts. Creative thinking is a habit anyone can develop. One of the rewards of developing this skill is a richer approach to problem-solving.

Whether or not you feel as if you have a natural talent for this process, you can build your capacity to think beyond the status quo. One way to boost creativity is by giving yourself the freedom to think without barriers. Allow yourself to be curious, ask questions, and entertain peculiar ideas. Inquisitiveness builds understanding, which makes it easier to relate to others, feel confident, and think positively.

As curiosity pilots you toward fresh perspectives, you will find it easier to engage in creative thinking and problem solving. Do not be afraid of thinking more daringly. The very act of dreaming up unrealistic ideas leads you to generate more rational solutions. As each idea encourages another, insurmountable problems will begin to feel more manageable.

Speak Up

Talking is one of the ways through which you process events in your life. Expressing what is on your mind, answering questions, and clarifying ideas allow you to sort through what happens on a daily basis. The cathartic qualities of talking can trigger positive shifts in your attitude.

Sharing your experiences with another person gives you the opportunity to expand your perspective. The act of contextualizing details for your listener can reveal thoughts that you had not been able to internally articulate. Hearing your situation out loud often leads to new ideas and possible solutions. It can make an obstructed view suddenly transparent. The end result of speaking up is a much needed mental release that settles your emotions, provides reassurance, and reduces feelings of isolation.

Be Wary of How You Interpret Text

Advancements in technology have evolved our language and reading comprehension in exciting ways. Things such as e-mail, text messages, and tweets have made impromptu writers out of people who, without technology, may never have written a word. The multitude of electronic correspondence options allows for an equal number of miscommunications. A very common and dangerous mistake is the misinterpretation of text—reading the wrong emotions into words and misconstruing a message's intent.

When you have an in-person conversation, facial expressions, body language, and syllabic emphasis communicate just as much as the words themselves. On the telephone, tone of voice and speed of words provide extra information and safety measures. The speaker, however, contributes tone instinctively (but at times deliberately) by choosing words that most accurately reflect the intended meaning. Verbal conversation allows the speaker to hear his or her own words and make immediate corrections to inadvertent or tactless remarks. The immediacy of conversation allows the speaker to recognize what comes out wrong and respond to how it sounds or is being perceived.

In today's rushing world, people type out immediate, raw responses on their phones and computers, often unaware of how their chosen words could be misinterpreted. Words with little context lack tone, and so the reader applies various connotations. The mind infers many things automatically, but they may not always be accurate. In order to avoid unnecessary confrontations, written conversations must be very specific.

Knowing this, the next time that you read a written message and think that someone is being abrupt or rude, consider whether that tone is intended or simply a shortcoming of the form of communication.

Practice Active Listening

Good listeners pay attention to what other people say instead of planning what they are going to say next. It takes a focused effort to develop this skill. But how does the effort benefit you? Effective listeners create a peaceful and understanding atmosphere that puts others at ease. Active listening encourages participants to open up to each other and respond with genuine feeling instead of exerting their effort to maintain positions and postures.

Imagine that you strongly disagree with a colleague and have spoken multiple times about the point of contention without actually coming to terms with anything. Neither of you may be listening to each other as much as mentally preparing to jump in with previously presented arguments to dispute the other person's perspective.

To actively listen, pay careful attention to the words being spoken and repeat back key points to ensure you've understood correctly. You might have heard other people use phrases such as "So, what I'm hearing is . . ." or "If I've got this right, you think. . ." This process makes the other party feel understood and more willing to listen to what you have to say.

Sometimes, conversations do not go well simply because you or the other person is preoccupied. When you want to raise a touchy subject or initiate a particular conversation, ask the other person if it is a good time to talk before you launch your speech. When someone approaches you or calls at an inopportune moment, anticipate the problem. Rather than half-heartedly listening, speak up, admit that you are unable to devote your full attention to the conversation at that moment, and suggest a better time. While active listening may not lead to agreement, it will make both parties feel more understood, which can lead to increased empathy and improved communication.

Stop Making Excuses

If you have ever made a mistake, you have made an excuse. Whether you say it out loud or keep it a thought, excuses provide a handy defense against guilt over your errors. Rather than serving as objective, forthright explanations, rationalizations typically blame others or outside circumstances for situations that did not work out as intended. A reflex reaction born of panic, such pretexts are cover-ups intended to make you feel more competent than you might otherwise appear.

What you must realize, though, is that there is nothing wrong with taking a misstep here and there. Mistakes mean that you are trying. You're challenging yourself and perhaps working toward new ideas or goals. Being able to accept errors as your own responsibility can lessen any consequences. When things truly go wrong, diminishing your involvement to lessen your liability is not worthy. Stop making justifications and take ownership of your mistakes. Instead of trying to reduce your responsibility for your circumstances, ask yourself what you should have done differently. Take a genuine look at your role in the situation. Forgive yourself for knee-jerk excuses, but make an honest appraisal of your circumstances, keep your expectations high, and make an effort to take full control of your actions and their consequences.

Live an Inspiring Life

Be as you wish to seem.

—Socrates

You are a gift to the world. You bring others joy, comfort, and hope, even if no one tells you so. The combined attributes of your demeanor and personality have never existed before and can never be duplicated—out of nearly seven billion combinations, you are unique. Every experience and consequence contributes to who you are. Sometimes the process is painful, but through the obstacles, you gain lessons and wisdom that enrich your life and the lives of those around you. You may struggle at times, but you can be restored and rejuvenated.

Never precede any description of yourself with the word "just." You are not "just" a woman or "just" a man or "just" a parent or "just" a kid or "just" any other role. Take pride in what you do and who you are to others and honor the unique attributes that you bring to the world. If you are still figuring out what those are and where you best fit, embrace the exciting potential of the journey. No matter what crossroads you face, you will learn and grow from every experience into a new and exciting mosaic.

Remember to respect your mind and your body. Love who you are and who you can become. Remember your best helpers: resolution, hope, and resolve.

Next Steps

Now you have one hundred tools that can chip away at the rough spots you encounter during your life. Some problems will dissolve like salt in water; others will persist like pebbles stuck inside your shoes. With tenacity, the toughest problems will wear away until they are as insignificant as a single grain of sand on a sun-soaked beach.

Make the most of these pep talks by rereading them when the rocks get in your shoes. Use these insights to enhance your strength, celebrate your individuality, and remind yourself that if you look hard enough, you can always find new ways to be optimistic. Believe that your efforts will be rewarded in ways you could never predict.

Coping with your struggles allows you to build the personal resources you need to carry on and grow. Your role is to find and appreciate the value of life's obstacles and use the skills you develop to respond in meaningful ways.

Good luck, and don't lose hope. Now turn back to the beginning of this book and read the dedication. You are not alone on your journey.